TOUCHED BY HEAVEN

ROBIN WOOD

TOUCHED BY HEAVEN

When God Sends Revival

ROBIN WOOD

AMBASSADOR INTERNATIONAL
GREENVILLE, SOUTH CAROLINA & BELFAST, NORTHERN IRELAND

www.ambassador-international.com

Touched by Heaven
When God Sends Revival

ISBN: 978-1-62020-295-1
eISBN: 978-1-62020-372-9

Printed by Bethel Solutions

Scripture quotations taken from the NIV.
Copyright 1973, 1978, 1984 by International Bible Society. Used by permission of
Hodder& Stoughton, a member of the Hodder Headline Group. All rights reserved.

Ambassador International
Emerald House
427 Wade Hampton Blvd
Greenville, SC 29609, USA
www.ambassador-international.com

Ambassador Books and Media
The Mount
2 Woodstock Link
Belfast, BT6 8DD, Northern Ireland, UK
www.ambassadormedia.co.uk

CONTENTS

To my ever-loving wife Shirley
- faithful in prayer -

Foreword

You will have noticed there's an 'R' in ChRistianity. There are several in fact, around which the Christian faith revolves: the Revelation of a great and gracious God; the Ruin of the human race through disobedience; Redemption through the blood of Christ; Rebirth by the Spirit of God; Repentance and faith in the Lord Jesus; the Return of the King to reign forever. There are other 'Rs' contemporary Christians have grown familiar with over the past fifty years that are now familiar: Reformation by the Word of God, Renewal by the Spirit, Restoration in the Church, etc. But there is another 'R' that we forget at our peril, Revival.

In this warm-hearted, easy to read and well-applied book, you will find a most helpful introduction to the vast and so encouraging topic of Revival. The author takes time to define his terms, telling us what Revival is not as well as what it is, and spells out the implications for the world, the Church and the individual believer. Scriptures are drawn on and explained; historical instances of Revival are used illustratively and applied practically, and in a devotional spirit. One can hear the author's *cri de couer*, his earnest entreaty to the Lord to 'do it again'.

So, if you are looking for a book to inform your mind, warm your heart, and call the Church to prayer and repentance, read on! For here is a challenge to us all to 'seek the Lord while he may be found', and 'give him no rest' till he revives his work not only in far away places with strange sounding names, but in Great Britain and Continental Europe especially. Touched by Heaven. May the result of this good book be just that indeed.

Dr Steve Brady
Moorlands College, Christchurch

Introduction

Many authors have prefaced their book with the phrase;" I never intended to write this book". I too would want to make this introduction, as it is absolutely true.

Almost as far back as I can remember I have had an interest in the subject of revival. At times, as my wife would testify, it has absorbed me to the extent of becoming almost obsessional. Other authors on this subject have made similar claims, which I fully understand. In the 1950s, in my youth I can remember stories of the revival in the Hebrides being recounted by visiting preachers in our home which gripped me with fascination. The interest has continued over the years as I eagerly read any book related to the subject and would travel any reasonable distance to hear first-hand accounts.

In 1988, the vast amount of material which I had accumulated on the subject, found an outlet when I was invited to give a series of lectures to both external and internal students at Moorlands Bible College, where I was a staff member. The lectures were entitled "Fire from Heaven" and over a period of ten weeks I sought to explain the nature of revival both from an historical and scriptural viewpoint and answer some of the questions raised about it. I was subsequently asked to go to Thailand and give this series of lectures at a Bible College. Other invitations followed both at home and overseas and on more than one occasion it was suggested to me that some of the material should be put into print.

In 1992 God took my life in a different direction and we went to work in Thailand for the next three years. On returning to the United Kingdom I was appointed Field Director for Home Evangelism (formerly Christian Colportage Association) where I worked with evangelists across the country. Health issues forced me to retire from this work in 2007 and since then it has given me opportunity to reassess the situation and with the aid of modern technology put the material into a form which could be read by a wider audience.

There are two reasons why I feel that now is the time to write this book. The first concerns the general ignorance about the subject found amongst many Christians today. The word "revival" is spoken about in a casual form with no real understanding of its solemnity and importance. Several times I have been in churches where something along these lines has been said; "Let's put out more chairs this evening in case revival breaks out!". Revival is a serious subject and those who have experienced it speak only of it with quiet reverence, knowing they have been touched by God Himself. It is for this reason I have gone out of the way to give a definition of revival, it may not be complete or adequate but I hope it will help the reader to think seriously about the subject.

The other reason is the need of the hour which I have outlined in the final chapter. The church and ultimately the nation needs to know that touch of God again in revival and it is my prayer that some of my words will stimulate others to pray for a mighty move of God once again.

A story is often told (in varying forms) and I have no idea whether it is true but it illustrates a point. A man was standing over the grave of William Booth, founder of the Salvation Army and was heard to be praying aloud these words; "Please God, do it again!". That is a prayer I hope will result from this book.

I would like to pay tribute to the following authors who have written on the subject of revival, and I can only stand in their shadow: J. Edwin Orr, Leonard Ravenhill, Arthur Wallis, Brian Edwards and Colin Whittaker, their works have inspired and challenged me over the years and I commend them for further reading.

Finally, I would like to thank my former colleagues at Moorlands Bible College, for their encouragement and help in urging me to write this book.Also,Dr.Steve Brady, the current principal for writing the foreword and for making helpful suggestions. I must also thank my wife Shirley for her support, patience and prayers as I have spent time putting this all together.

Robin Wood
2014

Chapter 1

Why Revival?

1945 – The War was drawing to a close, to the relief of everyone. After the years of darkness, at last there seemed reason for hope again. People's minds were filled with plans, not just to see this terrible war brought to its conclusion but also for the future. In spite of the optimism, it was however still wartime, which meant constant restriction in almost every way of life and so no immediate, foreseeable end to the rationing of food.

I was born during the War, and my earliest recollection from childhood was during that time. I was brought up under those conditions of rationing and although as a child I never suffered from them, I never however had opportunity to enjoy luxuries such as fruit or sweets, to me they just did not exist. This was all to change when we as a family were introduced to some kindly American servicemen and they presented me with an incredible new commodity, a bar of chocolate! At first I had no idea what to do with it, but after negotiating the silver wrapper, it soon found its way into my mouth. The affect I am told was startling, a totally new, delicious taste had been discovered. The bar was devoured in minutes with evidence of its existence being left all around my face. In some strange way, in spite of my age at the time, the taste of that chocolate bar has remained with me ever since, which may well account for my peculiar interest in chocolate to this day.

I tell this story to illustrate how, almost everyone after tasting something new and delicious will desire after more and sometimes even go to great lengths to obtain that which has pleased them.

In the church there are many things that thrill us, bless us and encourage us. Conversions will thrill us, as will healings, praise and worship will bless us, church growth and unity of Christians will encourage us, but if we have tasted revival we will know there is something more and long after it with all our hearts.

Few have been privileged to taste revival first hand, but those who have, bring a completely new dimension to church life, which makes much of our enthusiastic activity appear superficial.

In a small Irish village, the church planned and prayed for God to work in their community for thirteen years. A mission had been planned, but God made it very clear that the timing was not right. They continued to pray, until clergy and laity together realised it was God's time to move. A series of meetings were planned in the church and they continued to pray. During one weekend some of the leaders were away from the church with the young people and after the evening session together when most were in bed, a few began to pray. As they prayed so God met with them in ways they had not expected, they wanted to pray for the forthcoming mission but they became overwhelmed with a sense of God's presence. Instead of praying for others, first the leaders, then others all round the room began to confess their sin. This was not something planned or ever done before, it was all spontaneous and enveloped in the presence of God, it did not seem harmful or out of place.

The shallowness in the lives of some who had been Christians for many years came to the surface that night, relationships that had been broken and marred for years were mended, pride and ambition were trampled underfoot as they realised something of the holiness of God. As this group of Christians prayed and rejoiced together, so others in different parts of the building were stirred out of their beds and inexplicably drawn down to this unannounced meeting and they too were faced with the same experience. It would not be an exaggeration to say that no sleep took place that night, lives were transformed and the church would not be the same again.

When the mission eventually took place some weeks after this event, almost the same thing happened again. The planned programme was often thrown to one side as God came down and met with His people in very wonderful and personal ways. Many lives were turned upside down as sin was dealt with in Christian people. In one family, the father and son had not spoken to each other for years, but as God met with them there was a reconciliation and the long feud was buried. In just a few days more was accomplished for the Kingdom of God than in the past thirteen years altogether. News of the happening in the church travelled around the village, and as the curious came to see for themselves, so many of them were converted. The prayer meetings took on a new lease of life and as they prayed for individuals in the village, before they finished praying, they would be converted. One Christian leader was knocked up in the early hours of one morning by a young couple desperate to find peace with God.

I cannot explain these events, I only know they happened, I know some who were personally involved in them and I also visited the church within a month of their occurrence. This sort of thing cannot be planned in a church programme or worked up through any amount of emotional stirring because it is a taste of Heaven, it is revival and when you have tasted it you can only long and pray after more.

In the North of Thailand, Christians gathered at the Bible College from miles around for the annual convention. This year it was to be different, not in the Bible teaching or worship, but because God was to meet with His people.

How it started no one quite knows, but what is known is that in the early hours of the morning oil lamps were seen burning in all the tents about the campus. Some thought that the young boys were planning pranks but when the flaps of the tents were opened they were found to be on their knees before God confessing their sin. Over the next few days the campus seemed to be shrouded in a holy awe as God was at work amongst young and old alike. The effect on the community was staggering as Christians from all walks of life began to witness, with a vigour hitherto unknown. One schoolmaster was so challenged by his pupils who had been touched in this revival that he went to find out more for himself and was converted.

I have met many who God touched in that revival, including the schoolmaster who is now an evangelist, and in spite of the fact it was some years ago the effects are still felt in that area.

Revival is the most thrilling and wonderful experience that a church or community can undergo. Although testimonies of experience in revival may be different, they all concur that it is life changing in a way that nothing else inside or outside the church can match.

There is no substitute for revival, without it the church may well drift into complacency, become absorbed into the world, and lose its effectiveness.

Where is the church going today?

Ideas and schemes to charge the church with life proliferate today. Conferences proposing new methods and programmes take place with monotonous regularity. Charismatic leaders with unlimited new skills take the centre stage in the modern church, but to what effect?

Most of the resources being offered to the church are good and useful but we must ask what will be the end result of them all?

Will they produce a people of prayer? Will they bring men and women to their knees in repentance? Will they put holiness in living back on the agenda for the church? Will they so affect the church that society is radically changed?

The answer is that they may help the process but only God will bring about a revival with these results in reality. Revival will accomplish overnight what all our efforts have worked towards for years.

Revival is the answer for church growth, revival is the answer for social action, revival is the answer for missionary enterprise, revival is the answer for our financial problems, and revival is the answer for every generation.

So many things are happening within the church, but it still today bears little resemblance to the church after the Day of Pentecost and its impact on society is relatively small. Something must happen if the church is to be an effective force for the current and future generations. On the whole the church has become too enmeshed in its own political problems rather than being the light and salt in society as Christ envisaged. Power struggles and divisions plague the church on every level in all denominations both new and old. Entertainment has often replaced the aggressive evangelism of former days. No wonder so many from outside look in and mock our weak displays of Christianity. Other religions such as Islam have become very militant and captured the hearts of hundreds who having realised the emptiness of materialism have searched to fill the spiritual void in their lives.

As far back as 1989 a journalist wrote in a national newspaper these words, summing up the picture of Christianity as seen by so many outside of the church:

"The bland lead the bland. Christianity is only a sentimental song sung while we cut the cake of good deeds.

Church services have become cosy, kissing affairs and the parson acts like a game show host."[1]

He goes on to say:

"Europe is post Christian. This is not to say we are merely materialistic. We still support good causes, such as "Children in Need" and lead free petrol. But we do not claim that it is God and religion which prompt these urges. Our charity is more likely to be stirred by the telly spectacular, as Comic Relief showed, than by the Sermon on the Mount".[2]

Yes there is much good in the church, with many signs of new life within, but assessments like this must make us ask serious questions as to what we are really like.

It was a century ago that missionary Amy Carmichael had a vision of blind men and women going to Hell while the church sat around in groups making daisy chains. That powerful and challenging vision could well be applied to the church today. Something needs to happen and happen soon!

Methods and missions may have their part to play, but unless God blesses the church with revival, its future is very bleak. Society has no hope for changing, the church's hope for change is revival, and with the church changed through revival there is hope again for society.

---

1   Peter Mullen *Why Islam treats us with contempt* Daily Mail 31 March 1989
2   *ibid*

Revival is the Answer.

Revival may not be a popular theme as it may cut across our plans and programmes and to many it may appear just an evangelical dream unrooted in reality.

We have tried so much in our own strength and consequently failed hopelessly. We need to be honest enough to throw ourselves back on the mercy of God and ask Him to intervene in our situation. Revival is never man-made; it comes direct from Heaven with the co-operation of man.

As the prophet Jeremiah called upon the people of Judah to repent, he painted this graphic picture of their state before God.

"My people have committed two sins: They have forsaken me the spring of living water, and have dug their own cisterns, broken cisterns that cannot hold water."
Jeremiah 2:13

Once again God's people under the Old Covenant had turned their backs on God and followed in other ways in spite of all He had done for them. They had found the lifeless ways of other religions far more attractive than keeping in close relationship with God who is the source of all life. They had become like shepherds on the hillsides hewing out cisterns in the rocks to contain shallow stagnant pools of water. In other words they were guilty of "doing their own thing", they had bound themselves up with irrelevances which had become more important than true worship. This only led to dissatisfaction, as with cisterns that are broken the water runs away, so this way of life was meaningless and only caused problems for them.

The church today may not be following worthless idols, but many things have come before true worship of God and far too many Christians are running around in irrelevant circles of activity. The people of Judah needed an intervention from God, so do we in revival or we may suffer similar consequences to Judah of old.

Those who have tasted revival cry out for more! All our feeble efforts in the church mock us without revival! Revival is the only answer because of the state we have allowed ourselves to get in!

Does Revival Last?

It would be foolish to believe in this fallen world that revival would solve all our problems and create for us a utopia on earth, but it will answer many problems and more importantly bring us back in touch with God. There is however one question which is often asked concerning the nature of revival, that is, does it last and if it does not, why not?

The question is very relevant, as we can see from a cursory examination of church history that revivals have come and gone at regular intervals.

It is evident from Scripture and church history that revival is for just one generation. God comes to meet His people at their point of need at a particular time and it is for them alone. Sometimes it is localised to a particular church, sometimes it envelops a whole area and as church history reveals sometimes reaches out to a whole nation. The visitation may be for years, weeks or just a day but in that time God is able to accomplish His purpose for the people in that generation. It is also true to say that whilst the initial impact may be dramatic the effects of it continue on for years to come. As we pray for revival in no way can we rely on the revivals of the past or on the other hand expect revival coming to us to be relevant to the next generation. The blessing of God in one generation becomes tradition in the next and fossilises in the following, that is why every generation needs to seek God for revival.

There is another reason why revival often comes to an end. That is, human nature asserts itself and seeks to take over the work of God. Most revivals are spoiled in the end by over organisation, or ambitious men and women, or money becoming too important. Wesley felt that money was one of the greatest dangers to the working of the Spirit of God amongst His people. Satan is very subtle and he will seek to spoil the best work of God, he does not like revival and will seek to undermine it, sometimes through those who have been most used in it.

Physical exhaustion is the other reason I would give for revival coming to an end. Revival comes in three phases, the first is the build-up when the people pray for it to happen (in small or large numbers), then there is the peak when God dramatically meets them in power, then the on-going working out of that revival which may go on for many years. Revival in this sense does not peter out but continues on and it is just the peak that comes to a conclusion. The peak of revival is physically exhausting, sleep is often abandoned for days, people need attention, and in the presence of God the practical affairs of life take second place. It is exhausting as any who have experienced it will confirm, but worthwhile and something never to be missed.

Revival is for just one generation, that is why it is needed now!

Here are some brief accounts of how God has moved at different times, in different parts of the world in revival.

Cornwall 1851 – Reports of revival are received from all over the county. During the vicar's sermon in one parish church, someone in the congregation cries out for mercy. This is quickly followed by more cries from all parts of the church and soon preaching becomes quite impossible. Spontaneous prayer overtakes the congregation as one and another find peace with God in what the vicar himself describes as the presence of the power of God. Such scenes as these continue in the locality during the next three years.

Zaire (formally Congo 1949) – Revival breaks out on the Christian Church in this part of Africa. As they are overwhelmed with the presence of God, so they are convicted of sin. Much restitution takes place as those who have stolen take back property to the rightful owners. So much property is returned to one police station that notices have to be given out requesting people to collect what belongs to them. Relationships are restored, sin is rooted out and the local community knows that something different is taking place. The long term effect of this revival is a deeper sense of love and unity among the Christians.

Canada 1972 – Revival comes to parts of Canada. A pastor arrives at Winnipeg airport after hearing reports of the happenings. He asks a taxi driver to take him to church, this is the driver's response:

"The town is all upside down. The most extraordinary things are happening. Criminals are giving themselves up to the police. People don't want to do anything but sit in church. We are called out at night to take people to church in the early hours of the morning" [3]

Nagaland, North East India, 1976 – The tribes people in this largely unknown part of the world, first encountered the Gospel

3   Kurt Koch *Revival Fires in Canada* P.27 Kregel Publications

through American Baptist missionaries in 1871 and a church was established which spread through the vast network of villages. During the 1970s the cry "Send a great revival" went up across the church. 1976 saw the answer to these prayers when revival fires touched every church in Nagaland. The revival significantly changed both the lives of individuals and of the community. Eye witness account to this revival is told by a student from Nagaland in her thesis for Master of Theology degree at Fuller Theological Seminary.

The Reverend Chubba Ao, one of the leaders in the Naga church on a visit to Britain said, "The revival was like death coming back to life!" He went on to say : "When revival comes God's power is evident everywhere and this brings men and women to repentance".

One could go on, such are the accounts of revival, not just from the past but even around the world today, it is what the church in the West needs above all else. Whilst there have been localised movements in various churches, there are few alive today who have witnessed a major revival such as was experienced in East Anglia in 1920 and the Hebrides in 1949. We need it but do not deserve it, may we pray to hear words such as were given to the prophet Ezekiel :

"This is what the Sovereign Lord says, It is not for your sake, that I am going to do these things, but for the sake of the my holy name, which you have profaned among the nations where you have gone. I will show the holiness of my great name, which has been profaned among the nations, the name you have profaned among them. That the nations will know that I am the Lord, declares the Sovereign Lord, when I show myself holy through you before their eyes." Ezekiel 36:22-23

CHAPTER 2

"Revival is not..."

The meaning of words in any language can change from generation to generation and from circumstances to circumstances. It is the constant use of a language through speech and writing that keeps it alive, and as those who use it change so do parts of the language, sometimes obviously, sometimes very subtlety.

In the English language words frequently change their meaning and some by misuse in one generation take on an entirely new direction by the next, if they do not disappear altogether. A generation ago the use of the word "gay" would be applied to someone who was happy and bright, quite often a child. To use that word in the twenty-first century it can only have one meaning, totally opposite to its former as its use now applies to those with homosexual tendencies. The word in fact, like many others, has been taken to soften the stigma in society once felt by this section of the community.

In the nineteen seventies a television interviewer was asking people in the street if they could describe a "gay" person, a variety of answers ensued and out of the dozens interviewed only one made the homosexual connection. How the usage has changed; in twenty-first century United Kingdom this word could only be applied in this way, its former usage almost unthinkable!

A similar change of use has occurred with the word "revival" although not so obvious. The effects of this misuse has caused misunderstanding and in some cases outright error by some sections of the church.

Evangelical Christians are notorious for banding around words and creating a ghetto language of their own. It must be bewildering for a person from outside coming into the church for the first time to find that he needs a dictionary to understand all the new words being used around him. We are loose with our words, and most of us at one time will have been guilty of using words we do not understand, just to impress others. "Revival", whilst not a theological term has suffered this treatment.

It has been applied to almost any happening in the life of the church from crowds at crusade meetings and to evangelical conventions of all theological persuasions. It has even been used to describe lively prayer meetings especially where noise has been the predominant feature in some of the new church movements.

Although it may seem somewhat negative, the purpose of this chapter is to attempt to put the record straight, so that we are not misled about this term and miss its incredible implications.

My reasons and occasions for visiting a jeweller's shop are few and far between, but on those rare visits I have stood and watched with amazement as the jeweller plied his trade. It is especially interesting (and romantic) to watch a shy young couple going about the business of buying an engagement ring. Many trays of glittering gems are brought out for their inspection and then their eyes light up on one in particular. Maybe it is a diamond and the jeweller with a glint in his eye, and probably with some kindly words will then take out a black velvet cloth. The ring is then placed on the cloth, and what a difference it makes, away from all the other jewels it sparkles with new hues and can be seen for all its glory set against the black background.

It is therefore against a black background, I want to look first at the definition of revival from a negative viewpoint so that we might see it for what it really is, and desire after it.

There are four main misconceptions about revival that I intend to look at.

Revival is Evangelism

In the Synoptic Gospels (Matthew, Mark and Luke), the words of Jesus are concluded by each writer with what is known as the Great Commission.
Matt.28:16-20   Mark 16:15-18 Luke 24:45-49

Each of these passages give us the same message, "to go and be witnesses". It follows through to the Acts (1:8) when Jesus again charges the disciples to be "witnesses" when the Holy Spirit has come upon them. Paul and the other New Testament writers pick this up in some of their letters.

It would be true to say that the whole of the Acts of the Apostles is an account of this being worked out in practice by the early Christians. They had found that becoming a Christian was not a matter of assenting to a creed or following an example, but coming into an experience of the new life through the Risen Lord Jesus. These new Christians seemed to find it natural to speak about what had happened to them (that is being a witness) in every situation, taking all opportunities given to them. Christianity is not something to be kept to one's self, but it is to be shared and if it is not shared poses a real threat to the life of the church. The commission of Christ to every Christian is to be a witness and to every church to go with the Gospel.

Whilst this task is the lot of every Christian, there are those in the church who are given the gift of an evangelist (Ephesians 4:11). As with all the other gifts it comes from God and although He may use natural talents and abilities, it is out of His grace the gift is given and equally can be recalled. The task of the evangelist is to be a proclaimer, to constantly make the message known and the proof of this gift will be seen in the results. In many cases it is the faithful witnesses in the church who sow the seed and then the evangelist comes at the right time and reaps the harvest.

Evangelism, whether through the individual witness of ordinary Christians or through the gifting of a God ordained evangelist is part of the church's life. If it is not happening, something is wrong and the church in question is dying a slow and usually painful death.

Evangelism from the Acts to the twenty-first century has been evident as part of the church and will continue to be so until Jesus returns. It is not however revival!

Evangelism may precede revival, evangelism may come out of revival, evangelism will continue through revival (usually more vigorously), evangelism will continue after revival – but it is not revival!

One of the significant features of Evangelical Christianity in the nineteenth and twentieth centuries was crusade evangelism, sometimes referred to as mass evangelism. The word "crusade" is not considered politically correct in the twenty-first century but I use the word as it was commonly used at the time. The normal form of this evangelism is for a series of meetings to be convened, often at a neutral venue where the Gospel can be preached by an evangelist. In the nineteenth century it was used by Charles Finney, Moody and Sankey, Torrey and Alexander and others both in the British Isles and America. In the twentieth century, men like Gipsy Smith, Frederick and Arthur Wood, Tom Rees, Stephen Olford to name but a few have all conducted successful evangelistic crusades. Probably the best known evangelist of the twentieth century and in human terms the most successful, has been Billy Graham. His first city wide crusade was in Los Angeles in 1949, but many observers agree that the most significant was when he came to Haringey Arena, London in 1954. The crusade lasted for three months from March 1st, vast crowds attended, churches all over the country were stirred and hundreds were converted, who would subsequently affect the next generation of the church.

In the aftermath of the Second World War, and almost two decades of limited and largely ineffective activity by the church, it seemed that at last something was happening in Britain, but was this revival? A stirring yes, a new sense of direction, certainly, but it was not revival, it was crusade evangelism at its best.

Many Christians at the time anticipated that revival would come as a result of this crusade, but although so many good effects were felt by the church at large, revival did not come.

There are two reasons why crusade or mass evangelism is often confused with revival. Large crowds and activity are mistaken for revival

The first thought many Christians have when asked about revival is large crowds. It is true that at times of revival vast crowds are often drawn together. In 1742 in Cambuslang, Scotland, God moved on the church in mighty revival power. The revival was already in progress with many significant happenings when George Whitfield was called in to preach. On 6 July 1742, it is estimated that around 50,000 persons flocked to the hillside overlooking the Clyde for a communion service at which Whitfield preached. Whitfield himself said of the event:

"Such a commotion surely never was heard of, especially at eleven at night. It far outdid all that I ever saw in America."[4]

---

4   Arthur Fawcett *The Cambuslang Revival* P 114   Banner of Truth

It was said that for about an hour and a half there were scenes of uncontrollable distress, like a field of battle. Many had to be carried into the manse, like wounded soldiers.

Other revivals have however been relatively quiet and seemingly only affected a limited number of people, sometimes just one church in particular. The important feature of revivals is the unique sense of the presence of God and although vast numbers may be touched, crowds as often seen at crusade meetings are not a sign of revival.

The use of the word "revival" in America

The quotation that Britain and America are "Two nations divided by a common language" was allegedly said by Winston Churchill [5], although he was probably only quoting George Bernard Shaw.[6] It is true that many words used in daily speech on one side of the Atlantic have an entirely different meaning on the other side. This can sometimes be to the great embarrassment of visitors from the one country to the other. Revival is one such word that has different meaning generally speaking in America than in Britain.

In America revival meetings are sometimes advertised outside of churches. A notice recently observed read as follows: "Revival will take place in this church every evening at 8.pm, except Mondays and Saturdays". The Lion Handbook on *Christianity in America* shows a photograph of one such notice outside a church in Washington D.C. 1939. This notice reads, "Revival services now going on, public cordially invited."[7] These churches and many others may be carrying on evangelistic and other activities very successfully but it is not revival in the true sense of the word. Revival can never be organised, it comes from God in His time and purposes.

5   *The Times* 26th January 1987,
6   *1951 Treasury of Humorous Quotations*   Esar and Bentley
7   *Christianity in America* P.397 Lion Publications

Dr. Clifford Hill who has written much on the subject of revival says this:

"Revival is the pure work of the Holy Spirit. It cannot be manipulated. It cannot be brought about by organisations and campaigns, crusades or by any other man-made or man-centred activities however piously motivated. Revival comes about only through prayer, through openness to the Holy Spirit and through dependence upon God! When will evangelicals learn this?" [8]

The root of this misuse of the word stems back to Charles Finney (1792-1875), A man greatly used by God in revival. It was he who stated, "Revival is the result of the right use of appropriate means".[9] In other words if the right conditions are fulfilled, revival is bound to follow. Dr. Edwin Orr, probably the world's foremost authority on the subject comments on this point:

"Mass evangelism has developed techniques, but the general revivals of religion were not techniques but rather spontaneous movements. This confusion of revival with mass evangelism may be traced back to Finney who said that a revival is the result of the right use of appropriate means, a notion valid in evangelism but utterly false regarding the three general awakenings of Finney's lifetime – 1792, 1830 & 1858 – which were neither planned, promoted nor programmed." [10]

Finney was a great evangelist and revival followed him wherever he preached. He organised evangelistic meetings all across America and in many cases revival followed. God used this man and his methods, but applied again by different men in different circumstances they have not brought revival. An

---

8   Clifford Hill *The Way to Revival* Prophecy Today May/June 1986

9   *Lectures on Revival* Charles Grandison Finney. Lecture 1 – "What a revival of religion is."

10   Quoted by Gilbert Kirby in *Revival, then and now*, a lecture published by the Countess of Huntingdon Connexion, 24 October 1981

evangelistic mission or campaign may be the instrument God uses to bring about revival, but in itself it is not revival.

Finney made much stress on the human responsibility and freedom in his famous lectures on revival. Many have adopted his methods, called them "revival", but they have only been a form of evangelism. Dr. Martyn Lloyd-Jones in one of his sermons on revival spoke about those who try and copy that which has happened in past revivals.

"They have repeated them down to the smallest details. Again, they may have read Finney's book on revival, his lectures on this subject, and they have put into practice everything that Finney tells them to do. Finney promises that if they do them they will get revival so they have done it all, but there has not been a revival. They have done their utmost with all their techniques and methods, but there has been no revival. They may have had a number of conversions, but there has been no revival." [11]

If we are to understand the real meaning and purpose of revival, we need to disassociate the use of the word from evangelism of any sort.

Revival is Renewal

In the latter part of the twentieth century, the whole church scene, particularly in England changed. This was largely the result of what is generally known as the "Charismatic Movement" which brought all sections of the church a greater awareness of the work of the Holy Spirit. The main emphasis has been the importance of the Holy Spirit coming upon individual Christians for the purpose of power to witness, as in Acts 1:8. The term

---

11   Martin Lloyd-Jones *Revival, can we make it happen* P138 Marshall-Pickering

"the Baptism of the Holy Spirit", once used by Pentecostals and shunned by most other Christian groups became more widely accepted.

Along with the Baptism of the Holy Spirit, came the use of spiritual gifts as outlined by Paul in 1 Corinthians 12-14. The use of these gifts, once frowned upon as something peculiar to the Pentecostals, are now accepted in a wide variety of churches.

Worship has changed, once it was a choice between the formal liturgy and an informal "hymn sandwich". The Charismatic Movement has brought freedom in worship, with opportunity for members of the congregation to fully participate with songs, prayers, readings and many of the spiritual gifts. New songs have proliferated bringing an entirely new dimension to worship.

The history of the charismatic movement from the 1960s onwards in the British Isles has been well documented in books such as *The Spirit of Renewal* by Edward England [12] and there is no point in this book of going over in detail that same section of church history. However in order to cover the background I want to look at it from a personal perspective.

It was in 1963 as a young Bible College student, I first came across this new movement in the church. News that a curate, at that most conservative of evangelical establishments, ,All Souls, Langham Place, London, had received the baptism of the Holy Spirit and spoken in tongues swept through our college like a fire out of control. It was not long before fellow students of mine were also coming into this experience, much to the consternation of the college authorities who even placed a ban on students attending any Pentecostal or Charismatic type meetings.

There were two other significant events for me at that time.

---

12   Edward England *The Spirit of Renewal*   Kingsway

The first was the introduction of David Wilkerson's book, *The Cross and the Switchblade*[13] to this country. This book telling of a preacher's mission to the street gangs of New York, with all the problems of drug addiction and crime hit me like a bombshell. The impressive feature was the evidence of the miraculous and again the need Wilkerson emphasised for the baptism of the Holy Spirit. This was radical thinking for conservative evangelical students at a Bible College and it caused much heart searching.

The other factor was my introduction to a group of Christians, meeting not in a church building but in a community centre where they expected the gifts of the Holy Spirit to be exercised. This was the House Church movement in its embryo form.

Whilst I had and still have some difficulty in accepting the theological basis for some of the statements and practices of this movement, I have to be honest along with many others in the church and accept its challenge.

Perhaps the most important factor, and some would say difficult factor, to immerge from the Charismatic movement has been the development in some quarters from renewal to what has been called restoration, largely embracing the house church movement.

As the Holy Spirit was experienced by so many in a new way, the question was raised as to whether there should be a break away from the historic denominations. Many in fact did just this and the term "house church" was coined referring to those meeting in homes, schools, community centres and other places rather than in established church buildings.

---

13   David Wilkerson *The Cross and the Switchblade* Hodder and Stoughton

Andrew Walker in his book *Restoring the Kingdom*[14], aptly traces this development within the charismatic movement with its strengths and weaknesses, leaders and leadership style with all its attendant problems, its phenomenal growth yet constant division within its ranks.

This new part of the church continues to grow and in many areas interacts healthily with the historic churches, and has itself produced leaders with a wide range of ministry.

All of these developments, both within the historic churches and the many new ones, together with the growth experienced by some sections of the church do not constitute revival. There have been excesses and problems, but overall the effect of the charismatic movement on the church has been for good. It is a work of God, but falls short of revival!

Renewal has sometimes been compared to Abram's acceptance of Ishmael in Genesis, instead of waiting for God's best in Isaac. The great danger is for the church to settle for an Ishmael when God is yet to send an Isaac in the form of revival.

On Saturday 5 March 1988, many Christians came together in different parts of the British Isles to pray for the nation. During that day a word was given through David Noakes emphasising the need to move on from renewal to what God has in store for His people.

"What have you done with my Spirit? Did you not know what I wanted to do with my Spirit? I have been sending my Spirit amongst you many years for holiness, but you continue to sin; to lead you into repentance but you have chosen to substitute renewal; to witness but you have settled for entertainment. How can it be that I would send my Spirit among you and you would

---

14   Andrew Walker *Restoring the Kingdom*   Hodder and Stoughton

so fly in the face of all He wanted and you would turn to your own ways? You have been putting me to shame in the world. I wanted repentance and revival and to touch a lost world for whom my heart aches....."[15]

The developments of the 1960s onwards while not being revival could be laying the ground for revival. In 1936, the Pentecostal evangelist, Smith Wigglesworth spoke about a great revival that would come through the historic denominations which would far eclipse the Pentecostal movement itself. Renewal could be the forerunner to revival but it could also fossilise into just another movement to be recorded in the annals of church history.

Revival is a Stirring of the Emotions

One of the most common criticisms of revival is that it is just an emotional response to certain events. It is alleged that this has the effect of both attracting large numbers and these numbers themselves exaggerate the response in individuals.

Whilst this criticism in itself is an unfair assessment, it is absolutely true that when God works in revival power, emotions are stirred and sometimes most unusual things result. During the ministry of both Wesley and Whitfield frequently individuals were literally thrown to the ground under the power of the Holy Spirit.

In Ballymena, Ulster during 1859 as revival swept the province, it was said that strong crying and prayers were heard in the streets, and in almost every house, there was the manifestation of a Divine agent working mightily. One girl was so affected she appeared to be taken into the presence of the

15   David Noakes *Repentance and Return* Prophecy Today May/June 1988

Lord for nearly three hours and many other out of the ordinary events took place.

These events and many others in times of revival are well documented; emotional response is often, although not always, one of the results of God working. The emotional response which is so often seen as being revival is only one of its bi-products but it is not revival.

It is very difficult to understand why emotions in response to God should be so heavily criticised when they play such a large part on other areas of life. Take for instance sport, and see the emotions that are generated by supporters of an individual or team in many different games. It would be a strange and uncanny experience for the F. A. Cup Final to be played in complete silence; in fact it would be unthinkable. The supporters of both sides seem to get personally involved with their teams, which results in a high level of decibels being recorded from the Wembley stands, besides other unusual antics.

A few years ago a football match was played between two major sides behind closed doors, in other words in a football stadium with no supporters present. The state of affairs was imposed by one of the European Football bodies as a result of the unruly behaviour of supporters at a previous match. When this unusual match had been played, the players almost to a man commented that it totally lacked atmosphere with no-one present. Emotions play a very important part in sport, both in raising them among supporters and in encouraging those who are actually playing.

Equally in romance many different emotions are raised. The moment a young couple fall in love they experience a strange stirring within them. On the wedding day emotions are stirred all round, often more on the part of the couple's parents than the couple themselves, as they are usually too preoccupied with the day's events. Alone on the honeymoon, a feast of totally new emotions well to the fore, as their hopes and dreams are at last fulfilled. Emotions in these areas and many others of human experience are not questioned, why then should there be questions when the Holy Spirit touches an individual and they respond in an emotional way. God created our emotions and if He chooses to use them, then surely that is His prerogative.

The problem that critics seem to have, is not so much that a particular emotional response is from God, but that it alone is seen as revival and they focus on it.

Emotions may be stirred during a time of revival, those responses are part of the overall happening, but they are not revival itself.

In an earlier section, we have already mentioned about the large crowds which often result as revival occurs. It is true that when any crowd forms, people are stirred up in different ways and many critics would say that the response is only as a result of so many being gathered together.

This may be true in some cases, but in times of true revival we find people inexplicably drawn together by the Spirit of God. This was particularly the case in Whitfield's day, also in the Welsh Revival of 1904 and the Hebridean Revival of 1949. Observers spoke of an "unseen force" that drew the masses together. A reporter from the *Pall Mall Gazette* in London went to Wales in 1904 to report on the revival. He was amazed at what he witnessed and this is part of his report:

"There is something there from the other world. You cannot say whence it came or whither it is going, but it moves and lives and reaches for you all the time. You see men and women go down in sobbing agony before your eyes as the invisible Hand clutches at their heart. And you shudder..."[16]

Not only is it the Holy Spirit who draws them together but it is the Holy Spirit who does a work in an individual's life. When the Holy Spirit genuinely touches a person, he is changed and the results last a lifetime.

Crowds may come together in revival which may increase the emotional effect, but it is the work of the Holy Spirit in the individuals that is important and crowds alone are no mark of revival.

Jonathan Edwards who was used of God from 1734 onwards at Northampton, Massachusetts and other places in New England comments on experiences in revival in his work, *A Treatise concerning Religious affections* [17]

" The fact that affections are raised very high are no sign that they are true, the fact that there are great effects on the body are no sign, fluency and fervour are no sign, that they are not excited by us is no sign, that they come with texts of Scripture is no proof that they are real, that there is an appearance of love is no sign, religious affections of many kinds are no sign, joys following in a certain order are no sign, much time and zeal in duty, many expressions of praise, great confidence, affecting relations are no sign." He continues, "Gracious affections are from Divine influence. Christian practice is the chief sign to others and to ourselves."

A display of emotions alone, even if it is an obvious work of God is not revival, but they should not be despised when they do occur in revival.

---

16   William T. Stead *Pall Mall Gazette*
17   Jonathan Edwards *A Treaty Concerning Religious Affections* first published
          1746

Revival is a display of the Spectacular

Another common misconception is that revival is just about spectacular displays such as healing and other miracles. As with emotions, again it would be incorrect to deny their existence in revival and again it would be correct to say they may be a bi-product.

Some consider the greatest period of revival in the history of the church were the years 1858-9 when God first moved in America and then swept across the world. In America alone in one year over one million people were converted and another million revived in the churches, yet that revival was almost solely a time of prayer and there is no record of spectacular happenings other than conversions.

In other revivals, particularly in Africa and Indonesia there have been wonderful miracles, some beyond human imagination.

When God moves in revival it is spectacular, because primarily the church awakes from slumber and begins to act as God intended it. However spectacular displays may occur, they alone are no evidence of revival.

These are some of the common misconceptions about revival, and there may well be others. It is however important to understand them so that when we define revival itself, we may approach it without any preconceived ideas.

CHAPTER 3

What is Revival?

One of my favourite cartoons is the "Love Is" series where the simply drawn male and female characters are portrayed in all manner of circumstances, each to illustrate an aspect of love. These were very popular a few years ago and appeared in magazines and newspapers and I used to cut them out and give them to my wife who kept them in a scrapbook. We found they beautifully described different aspects of our life and love together.

I have the greatest admiration for the creator of this series, the late Kim Casali as she gave herself an impossible task, for who can describe what love really is? The impossible nature of this task no doubt ensured the perpetuation of these cartoons, now controlled by her son Stefano Casali.

There are so many angles to love, you can look at it from one angle and think you have it, and then you immediately see something quite different. It is one of those nebulous words where we have an understanding of its meaning, yet we have the utmost difficulty in describing it except in terms of experience.

When we look at the word revival we are faced with a similar situation, who can truly describe it? Yet so many have felt its warmth and action in their lives.

First of all I want to look at the word itself to see what is actually meant by it, then go on to look at the numerous definitions that have been given for it, and then to look at personal experience in it.

The word "revival" is used in many different contexts today. Dictionaries generally agree with definitions such as: "an act of reviving", "the return of life", or an intensive campaign to arouse religious fervour".

Let us look at the act of reviving. Implicit in this phrase is the notion that the object or person is either totally without life or very nearly in that state. Someone for instance who is fit, well and very much alive does not need to be revived, in fact cannot be revived. A person who has little life in their body certainly does need to be revived.

If a person has been drowning and is rescued by the lifeguard, when they come out of the water every attempt will be made to revive the one who almost found a watery grave. Massage, mouth to mouth resuscitation, application of oxygen and any other method as necessary will be employed by the skilled lifeguards to revive and bring the person back to life. If the attempt is successful, the person whose life was in danger will have been revived. That in terms of humanity is an example of revival.

It is used in other areas of life, not just in terms of human beings, objects are sometimes revived. I recently noticed an advertisement for a company who called themselves "The Kitchen Revival Centre". The task of this company is to sell new kitchens to replace old, worn out ones. When the totally new kitchen has been fitted out, it can be described as having been revived.

One also hears this word used in connection with political parties. It may be said that "there has been a revival of fortunes", in a particular political party.

During one springtime whilst on holiday in North Devon I found a good example of the use of this word. My wife and I were touring over Exmoor and through the beautiful coastal scenery of North Devon when we stopped at the picturesque town of Lynmouth. We have visited the town on several occasions in the past and as on those previous visits my mind immediately remembered the tragic disaster of the Lynmouth flood in 1952.

As a schoolboy I remember the shock and horror of it and how we had collected pennies in the classroom to contribute to the disaster fund.

On this visit however my eyes were drawn to a notice that described the Lynmouth Hydro Electric Scheme. The whole story of the disaster was described, how on the night of 12 August 1952 while the residents of the quiet fishing town were in their beds the great flood came. Over previous days it had rained hard and the waters had built up over the moors to such an extent that the rivers could not contain them. On that terrible night, what can only be described as a wall of water hurtled down the valley sweeping everything before it until an outlet could be found, that was Lynmouth! In seconds the town, its houses, shops, churches, bridges and, worst of all its people were swept out to sea. Many lost their lives on that fateful night.

The town has since been rebuilt and the poster went on to explain how new life had been brought to the town and how that same force of water had been harnessed in the development of the Hydro Electric Scheme. The heading on the notice read as follows: "A story of destruction, enterprise and *revival*." (my italics). Once this town had been destroyed and almost died; now it had been brought back to life and the very force used against it was now working for it, that is an example of revival.

When we use the term correctly in respect of the church (for it is to the church and not the world at large that revival comes), we have to assume that it is in a state without life, otherwise it would not need to be revived.

A healthy church does not need to be revived, it is when a church is without life and is so influenced by the world around that then it needs revival.

The Oxford Dictionary defines revival in our English language as "a reawakening of religious fervour". It is precisely that, in the power of the Holy Spirit, which an ailing church desperately needs.

Definitions of true Revival

As one reads books on the subject, one thing becomes plain; definitions of revival are legion. Every author seeks to define what is meant when we speak of Heaven sent revival. The problem is that they are each trying to define the indefinable, as we have already mentioned.

Most definitions are quite valid, but they tend to emphasise one aspect or another and are never able to encompass the whole. In making this statement I know I am immediately setting myself a trap for when I try and define the word. I fully recognise this, but my definition along with those from many godly authors, some of whom know it from experience, should I trust, build up as complete a picture as possible. It is important that we have this understanding, so we might pray positively and more effectively towards it.

As I have studied the subject for years, read on it extensively, and talked with anyone who has had contact with it, I have summarised my thoughts with this definition.

"It is a sovereign intervention by God upon His church, at a particular point in history, in a visible and powerful way that can only be described as out of the norm."

Let me now expand on this definition before looking at what others have to say on the subject.

It is a sovereign intervention by God.

This, I feel, is the most important statement we can make about revival – it comes from God!

Revival is not something that can be manufactured or manipulated; it is entirely dependent upon God. Revival comes when God chooses, and in one sense there is absolutely nothing men can do about it. God is sovereign and it is His prerogative alone for Him to intervene in the life of the church.

We certainly can pray for revival and ask God to do it in our time, but the "when" and "where" of revival are in His hands. Why did God choose to sovereignly come down in power upon the church in the island of Lewis off the Scottish coast in 1949/52? Why did He not do the same thing in mainland Scotland or across the rest of the British Isles? The answer is, we do not know, we have to leave it to God.

Why is it that God is blessing the church in parts of Asia, Africa and South America in a way that the Western world is not experiencing? We can hazard a guess, but a guess it will only be, for it is God's choice of time and place.

Many faithful Christians, like the late Arthur Wallis, who wrote *In the Day of Thy Power*[18], prayed all their lives for revival and it did not come. Has God heard their prayers? He certainly has, but how He answers is up to Him.

We can put the same question "why" against many of the

---

18   Arthur Wallis   *In the Day of Thy Power*   Christian Literature Crusade (1956)

incidents of God's blessing in the Bible and we have to answer the same, it was God's sovereign intervention.

Upon His Church

If it is up to God when and where He works, who is it then that He moves upon when He comes in revival blessing? Unquestionably it is the church, God's people that He comes to in this way. It is after all the church that needs reviving, not the world as that is already spiritually dead. It is the church that God loves and cannot bear to see in an ailing state that He comes upon in sovereign power.

It needs to be mentioned at this point that when God touches His church, inevitably the community at large will be affected. It is sometimes this effect upon the world in general that is seen as revival, strictly this is not the case, it is the church that God touches with revival and then the church affects the world.

Dr. Edwin Orr, one of the foremost authorities on this subject, speaks of God's work upon the church as revival, and the outcome in society as an awakening.

In point of fact the two are often so linked they cannot be seen apart, as in the days of Wesley and Whitfield, but we need to understand that revival as such comes solely to the people precious to the Heart of God – His Church.

At a Particular Point in History

Revival is not something vague or mystical, it is not something that happens in the spiritual realm alone, it is an event in history. It can be dated precisely in most cases, and it is witnessed by many and certainly for the past three hundred years is well documented.

There is often a notion that revival is vague in the sense that it might be happening or on the other hand it might not! This view is due to lack of understanding as to the nature of revival.

The revivals of the past are as historically well documented as any of the great battles such as Hastings or Waterloo. No question is asked about the accuracy of those events, and equally the accuracy and actual timing of revivals is beyond question.

When we study revival, we are studying fact; we are looking at a point in church history when God actually intervened with remarkable results.

The more recent the revival, the more that is written about it, and from the early days of the Evangelical Revival in the eighteenth century, very accurate records of events have been kept. God is so wise in the choice of his servants. It was Wesley, a tutor at Oxford University, a man meticulously accurate in everything that he turned his hand to, that God used to spearhead revival. Wesley kept the most accurate of journals, all of which are available today. Not an event or incident is unrecorded and left to speculation, it is all written down for our benefit.

Whitfield likewise kept journals which together with the secular historical records give an accurate picture of revival in his day.

At later revivals we have another source which verifies the events of the day; the newspapers. In 1858/9 the newspapers reported extensively the revival in both America and the British Isles. During the 1858 revival in New York reporters raced from one prayer meeting to another by horse and cab, and daily reports of numbers at meetings appeared in the papers.

I have a copy of the *Belfast Newsletter* 250th anniversary souvenir edition and in the listings of significant events in Ireland over two hundred years, 1859 is listed as "The Year of the Great Revival". In more recent times it has caught the eye of the media, such as in Asbury, Kentucky in 1970.

Revival is fact, God touches His church and human affairs in many areas are affected.

In a Visible and Powerful Way

In the just the same way as we have already stated revival is a historical fact, so also is it something that is visible in its manifestations and very powerful.

When God works in an individual's life, it is in the heart, between God and man alone and this is equally so in times of revival. There are however several ways by which evidence of revival is visible.

Physical manifestations

In revival as the lives of individuals are touched, many and varied are the physical manifestations. The power and presence of God is so great that men and women are often swept to the ground, cry out before Him as they realise their sin, appear to be lost in another world and sometimes in revival physical sickness is healed instantaneously and individuals are delivered from the power of Satan.

During the Kentucky revival of 1800/1 as the Spirit of God came upon the vast crowds so the scene resembled that of a battlefield. The noise was overwhelming as men and women cried out to God and many were just thrown to the ground in a motionless state. One witness said that a "strange supernatural power seemed to pervade the entire mass..."[19]

People are Drawn Together

When God works in revival people are drawn together, sometimes out of curiosity, but more often than not they are drawn by the power of God. This was certainly the case in Wesley and Whitfield's day, so it was in Wales as Daniel Rowlands preached in 1735, and again in 1904 when revival broke out, each morning as dawn broke the sound could be heard across the valleys of the footsteps of young and old as they were drawn together to pray.

The effects of revival are visible and when it happens in a church the community around cannot help but take notice.

As well as visible, it is also powerful, so much so its force can be felt. In Northampton, New England 1734, Jonathan Edwards reported that visitors coming to the town were nearly all affected by the wonderful atmosphere, and many went away under conviction of sin. In 1735, the whole population of the town had seemingly been affected by the revival, it could not be avoided.

The force in question is the presence of God; can there be anything more powerful?

It is Out of the Norm

The events of revival are not normal for church life. There are certainly supernatural occurrences which are obviously out of the norm, but there is another reason.

---

19   Mendall Taylor *Exploring Evangelism* P142, quoted by W. Pratney in *Revival* P115 Whitaker House

We have already made mention that revival comes when a church is ailing, because it needs reviving. It is because of the very state the church has brought upon itself that only God's intervention is the answer. Therefore as the church is ailing, it is also complacent, it is inward looking, it is compromising and this is sadly the way it is often seen and this is accepted as the norm. When God breaks through all of these attitudes have to change which means that God is working in what is considered to be outside of the norm.

If God's people really desire revival, they have to be prepared to change because that certainly is what happens when revival comes to the church of God.

There are no doubt gaps in my definition of revival and it is therefore helpful to look at others as well.

One of the most quoted and succinct definitions is from D.M. Panton when he says:

"Revival is the inrush of God's Spirit into a body which threatens to become a corpse"[20]

This emphasises again the state of the church which needs revival, a body, that is a New Testament term (1 Cor.12) for the church, which is almost dead. Into that weak and faint body, the Spirit of God breathes and life with all its manifestations follows.

Colin Whittaker, gives one of the most comprehensive commentaries on revival in his book *Great Revivals*. He says:

"By revival we mean those special seasons of divine visitation when God the Holy Ghost quickens and stirs the slumbering church of God. Believers are set ablaze for Christ and the power of God is so manifest in prevailing prayer and anointed preaching of the Gospel that the most hardened and sceptical

---

20   Quoted by Colin Whittaker *Great Revivals* P15-6   Marshalls

unbelievers are brought under great conviction of sin, leading in turn to genuine repentance and saving faith in the Lord Jesus Christ, through His death on the cross and resurrection."[21]

Arthur Wallis gives this neat summary of revival:

"Revival is such a display of God's holiness and power that often human personalities are overshadowed and human programmes are abandoned. It is God breaking into the consciousness of men in majesty and glory."[22]

He also comments in *Rain from Heaven*:

"It is essentially a manifestation of God. It has the stamp of deity upon it, and this even the spiritually uninitiated are quick to recognise."[23]

Another well-known preacher from a previous generation, J.D. Drysdale, gives this definition:

"It is a renewed interest in religion after indifference and decline; a reanimation from a state of languor, a voluntary and determined return to first things and a whole-hearted honouring of God. A revival is not merely the stirring of people's emotions but it is a mighty manifestation of the mighty power of God turning men and women of every walk of life from their sins to a life of God-glorifying and whole-hearted sacrifice and service."[24]

We could fill a book with definitions, but those mentioned should begin to set the scene in order to get that greater understanding of what God intends by revival.

---

21   Colin Whittaker *Great Revivals* P21 Marshalls
22   Arthur Wallis *Rain from Heaven* P15 Hodders
23   ibid P17
24   Quoted by Gilbert Egerton *Flame of God* P14 Ambassador Publications

It is not possible to bring them all together in adequate summary form but I have sought to bring my thoughts together on this subject in this way.

"It is a sovereign intervention by God upon His church, at a particular point in history, in a visible and powerful way that can only be described as out of the norm."

Our definitions may overlap, and even at times disagree, however all serious students of the subject would agree that it is a supernatural phenomenon, depending on the sovereign, supernatural work of God.

Testimony of Revival

The best definitions of revival are from those who have actually experienced it. When a person describes what happened it makes all of our definitions seem cold and clinical.

There were, even during the latter half of the twentieth century, Christians alive who could speak of first-hand experience of the Welsh Revival in 1904/5. It was a delight to speak with them, the very mention of the subject lit up their faces and the fruit of their experience was a lifelong labour for God. Sadly, we no longer have this resource today.

It seems that a person who experiences true revival is never the same again. When revival breaks out, God becomes central in man's thoughts and every part of their lives are affected. In the Hebrides, the late Duncan Campbell described the revival "as a community saturated with God."

I talked at length with an evangelist from Zimbabwe who had experienced revival first hand in many African countries,

He said, "When God comes down in revival, things are bound to change."

David Brainerd, son- in- law to Jonathan Edwards, spent the latter part of his short life (he died at the age of 29) as a missionary to the North American Indians. He laboured and prayed alone with the Indian community until God sovereignly lit a flame that spread like a forest fire amongst them in Pennsylvania. In 1745, he wrote of that outpouring of God's Spirit in his diary:

"The power of God seemed to descend upon the assembly like a mighty rushing wind and with an astonishing energy bore down all before it. I stood amazed at the influence that seized the audience almost universally, and could compare it to nothing more aptly than the irresistible force of a mighty torrent."[25]

When revival comes, the evidence of the presence of God is such that lives are changed instantly and the effects last a lifetime.

In John Gillies book *Historical Accounts of Revival*, which is a classic work on the subject, giving insight to the way God worked in generations past, recording information which otherwise would largely be lost, there is in the Appendix a wonderful account of revival in a community and its overall effect. It is the account of revival in the Scottish town of Kilsyth in 1839, the preacher Rev. W.C. Burns was God's instrument on this occasion and it is recorded in the following words:

"The state of society is completely changed. Politics are quite over with us. Religion is the only topic of interest. They who passed each other before, are now seen shaking hands, and conversing about the all-engrossing subject. The influence is so generally diffused, that a stranger going at hazard into any house would find himself in the midst of it."[26]

---

25   Quoted by Arthur Wallis *Rain from Heaven* P17 Hodders
26   John Gillies *Historical Collections of Accounts of Revival* P558 Banner of Truth

This paragraph is a definition, description and testimony of what happens in revival, that is true revival!

We cannot dictate to God how or when He will work, we can however look to the past and to some extent the present and see that God has come down on His church in power, this has been witnessed and accurately recorded for ours and every subsequent generation. When the church of our generation is in a state that resembles little more than a corpse, we can only pray that God will again have mercy and send revival on His people.

If asked to explain what is meant by revival to a person with no knowledge of the subject, I would use these words:

"It is an emotional outburst from God, when He can no longer restrain His love for His people as He sees their state in this world. He allows a fraction of Heaven to be poured out upon them on earth"

CHAPTER 4
Features of Revival

Definitions, for all their accuracy, can sometimes be misleading, and usually when one is asked to describe an object or experience the focus is upon the features of that object or experience. We have already made mention that definitions of revival are often inadequate and still lead to misunderstanding as to the true nature of revival.

The question one quite validly might ask is, "How do I know when revival happens and what are its features?"

In this chapter we shall seek to answer that question.

At the outset it must be stated that we cannot specify what God will do in revival. In one generation He may work in a particular way, at another time in a totally different way. A future revival may be worked out in ways different to the past and may even be beyond our imagination, that is God's prerogative.

In 1858 when revival swept across North America, it was primarily a movement of prayer. God called His people together to pray and it was at the prayer meetings that God did His work. Hundreds were converted at and through those meetings without hearing a word of a sermon preached. Some thirty years previous, God was using Charles Finney across the same nation but this time hundreds were converted through preaching. There was a mighty anointing of the Holy Spirit upon Finney when he preached, even his wife confessed that she was quite terrified when the power of God came upon him when he preached – standing there like a mighty angel wielding the flashing sword of judgement.[27] It was the same nation and the same God at work, both were experiences of revival. As we look at revival however there are common denominators right across church history; and it is those we examine as features of revival. On their own they do not necessarily constitute a revival, but combined with the power of God that cuts across normal church life, it may well be the case.

In a study of all revivals, it would seem that there are three factors common to them all. They are (1) Prayer (2) The fear of God, and (3) Conviction of sin and repentance.

1 - Prayer

Whilst we cannot dictate to God about revival, there is one feature we are bound to see in them all, that is prayer. Every account of revival gives record of it being soaked in prayer, usually before, during and after.

In 1949, in the Scottish village of Barva on the Isle of Lewis, it was two sisters who prayed for God to come down in revival power. The older sister was Peggy Smith, she was eighty four years old and blind, her sister Christine was eighty two and crippled with arthritis. Their heart was set on seeing God move and for years they did not leave their post at prayer until their faithfulness was rewarded. One morning in 1949, God clearly showed these ladies who had such an intimate relationship with Him, that revival was near. The rest of the story is history, of how God mightily came to that village and many others on the island, confronting men and women everywhere with His presence.

Prayer continued through the course of the revival, not in a ritual observance through weekly meetings but whenever

27　　Colin Whittaker *Seven Great Prayer Warriors* P95 Marshall-Pickering people came together they prayed, and often they were drawn together just to pray. Those times of prayer were so powerful, on one occasion when a man prayed the whole house shook; often people were converted in prayer meetings or as a result of them.

The Welsh Revival of 1904/5 is perhaps one of the most well-known. Significant event as this was, it was only part of what God was accomplishing across the world. It seems from the turn of the century, hearts had been set praying in anticipation of such an awakening.

Edwin Orr makes this observation: "The early twentieth century evangelical awakening was a worldwide movement. It did not begin with the phenomenal Welsh Revival of 1904/5. Rather its sources were in the springs of little prayer meetings which seemed to arise spontaneously all over the world, combining into streams of expectation which became a flood of blessing, in which the Welsh revival became the greatest cataract."[28] There are many accounts of prayer meetings coming into existence during the early days of this century in a quite spontaneous manner; this surely was the Spirit of God preparing the ground for the harvest to come.

Jesse Penn-Lewis who was herself in the Welsh Revival, when looking at its origins observed that in Melbourne, Australia, 1901, there were fifty missioners holding services at fifty different centres in the city, whilst forty thousand praying souls met in two thousand homes for home prayer meetings, encircling the city with prayer. Many met for half nights of prayer, and Melbourne was moved from end to end by the mighty moving of the Spirit of God.[29]

Like the Hebridean Revival later, so the Welsh Revival was

---

28   J Edwin Orr *Evangelical Awakenings in Eastern Asia.* P13 Bethany Fellowship
29   Jessie Penn-Lewis *The Awakening in Wales* P18 Overcomer Literature Trust

born in prayer, which continued through its course and beyond. Examination of other revivals would reveal the same pattern; prayer is a prominent feature of revival.

John Wesley once commented that "God does nothing in this world redemptively except through prayer."

Whilst prayer is an essential element for revival, it must however be stated that prayer alone in not a guarantee for revival. The "when" and "where" of revival belongs to God alone, countless thousands have prayed to God throughout their lives for revival and gone to their graves without seeing it. Never could it be said that such prayer meetings have been wasted, it is the matter of timing on God's programme for His church.

A Bible College lecturer known to me once made this succinct statement: "Revival seems always to have been preceded by prayer, but, much prayer may not necessarily produce revival."

This is absolutely true, there is a dichotomy about prayer and revival, on one hand without prayer there cannot be revival, and on the other hand prayer cannot produce revival. This is the wisdom and sovereignty of God which has to be accepted in all matters relating to revival. In fact it could be said that the unpredictability in the coming of revival; is a sure sign it is of God, not man.

More will be accomplished across the world by a praying church than all the politicians in the world, and we can take encouragement that when the church prays seriously and spontaneously, maybe revival is waiting in the wings. There is great power when God's people pray, hearts are stirred, sinners convicted, impossible tasks are completed. Mary, Queen of Scots was said to fear the prayers of John Knox more than the sound of marching armies. Daniel touched the very heart of Heaven and encountered the Arch Angel Michael himself as he interceded for his nation (Daniel 9&10). Every man or woman of God who has accomplished anything in this world, has first been a man or woman of prayer.

In recent years the most notable move of God has been in South Korea where thousands have come to faith in Christ. Churches across that nation are bursting to overflowing, with some of the largest in the world in the capital Seoul. Pastors and church leaders say without exception that prayer is the key.

All over the country thousands meet daily for prayer early in the morning, whilst others are found for days at a time seeking God on the dozens of "prayer mountains".

Prayer is one of the marks of revival, God's people must pray if they want to see God move once again.

2 - The Fear of God

In the year 739 BC the young Jewish courtier Isaiah, experienced something that was to totally change his life and set the framework for his future ministry. Where it actually happened is open to speculation, but what happened is not, for he was ushered into the presence of God. In that moment (however long it was, it must have seemed a lifetime!) he felt the holiness of God both by sight (Isa.6:3) and by sound (Isa. 6:4) which made him realise his own state of uncleanness (Isa. 6:5).

Isaiah's description of that experience and its affect upon him is very similar to that experienced by men and women in revival. In revival the presence of God is so real that one cannot escape His holiness.

This is another feature of revival, the fear of God, an awesome awareness of His presence. You can actually feel the presence of God in times of revival which results in lives of Christians being changed and sinners coming under conviction.

Is it possible to feel the presence of God? I see no reason why this should not be the case, after all you can certainly feel the presence of evil. As you walk down the streets of some of our larger cities, the evil is all around, you feel unclean even walking through and you want to wash away the dirt. In some cultures where occult practices are normal, evil may be sensed when entering a building or room. If evil can be experienced in a tangible way, surely it is not beyond Almighty God to make His presence felt. It was in fact the Puritans in the seventeenth century who use to speak in hushed terms of the "felt presence of God".

One of the great features of revival is that unique and intense awareness of the presence of God. Just as in the day of Isaiah, so when God comes down, His presence is felt and numerous records verify this for us.

In 1727, a remarkable revival took occurred in Germany which ultimately affected the world. The followers of the reformer Jon Hus (1374-1415) became known as the Moravians. They were scattered over Europe and at the beginning of the eighteenth century found themselves to be a persecuted people. Their land and property was seized and they were pushed from one state to another without finding refuge.

In 1722, a group of these refugees, led by Christian David arrived at the estate of the wealthy, nobleman Count Ludwig von Zinzendorf. He was a committed Christian and together with his wife they decided to open their estate to these "Moravian Refugees". On Zinzendorf's estate a community known as

"Herrnhut" (meaning the Lord's watch) was formed, but sadly it was not long before disunity set in between the members. Zinzendorf sought to bring them together and on 12 May 1727 an "agreement of unity" was drawn up and the community as a whole recommitted itself to God and each other.

It was just three months after this time of reconciliation on 13th August that God met the community in a wonderful and remarkable way. The Spirit of God fell on them in such a way that they were all affected including the children. The power and presence of God was so evident that witnesses commented that they hardly knew whether they were in Heaven or on earth. Lives were totally changed from that moment on, a prayer meeting commenced that was to continue for one hundred years, missionaries went out all over the world and John and Charles Wesley were greatly influenced by them.

In Northampton, New England 1734, during the time of Wesley and Whitfield, in Finney's day, in 1859, during the Welsh Revival and every revival whether large or small, the presence of God has been felt in such a way that lives are never the same again. It is the fear of God; that awareness of His holiness and our unworthiness that men and women experience in revival.

Such events are not just confined to previous eras, there are many accounts of this happening in recent times. Here is part of an account from one Christian leader when he was himself a student at Bible College:

"It was supposed to be the usual morning chapel hour before the start of an intense day of Bible College lectures. Today, however, was not the usual. Across the room, students and staff alike were falling on their knees before God. A deep and intense sense of His presence was amongst us. I lay prostrated on the floor before Him, crying out that what we were now experiencing would continue and intensify until the church of God worldwide would feel the power of His Presence."[30]

This experience was by no means isolated, as I know personally of other Bible Colleges during the 1960s where they experienced something similar, so much so that the normal lecture programme had to be suspended. I was present myself at a college chapel service in the 1980s when God moved in such a way that the silence was almost tangible. As members of staff we were not sure how to handle the situation and had to take the step of abandoning lectures for the day. Those who were students that day never forgot the experience and now established in ministry will refer back to it being a major landmark in their Christian journey.

In almost every revival we find that men and women have been prostrated before God, because His presence has become so real. Sadly God is often treated so lightly, almost as if He were just another of our friends. When His presence is really felt there is only one place for us, on the ground "face down" as we are aware of His holiness.

In 2 Chronicles 5, we have an account of the dedication of the Temple as made by Solomon for the Lord. At the height of the worship (v.13), "The Temple of the Lord was filled with a cloud", in other words the presence of God was felt in their midst. The result was (v.14) that priests could not perform their service – because of the presence of God. That is what happens in revival, the presence of God stops our normal, legitimate activity, as it is felt all around.

There are churches where this has happened, and it appears as if they have been enveloped with a cloud as God's presence

---

30   Bryn Jones *Suddenly all Heaven Broke Loose.* Restoration magazine July/
        August

has come down. It is very much felt and affects those who experience it, emotionally and physically, but above all in their relationship with God.

One of the features in some churches has been the so-called, "slaying in the Spirit", where individuals fall to the floor when someone has prayed with them. This is often organised and in the main this has nothing to do with prostration before God in revival. When God moves it is a spontaneous work, and individuals usually fall on their faces as with the apostle John when he met the risen Lord on Patmos Island (Revelation1)

The presence of God is one of the very real evidences of revival, it is God coming to His people and that people being totally changed.

3 - Conviction of Sin and Repentance

The other feature common to all revivals is the conviction of sin which leads to repentance. This we know happens when a person becomes a Christian. It is one of the activities of the Holy Spirit to convict in regard to sin (John 16:9) which consequently leads to repentance and faith in Christ. In time of revival as we have already seen it is primarily the church that is affected and when God comes in such power Christians are convicted of sin in their lives.

When God touches His church in revival, His people as they are faced with His presence cannot but be aware of His holiness. Just as with the young man Isaiah when faced with God's holiness, His utter purity, they are made aware of their own unworthiness and sinful state. If God's presence is real, it must bring about this effect, for Christians of whatever maturity still commit sin, no-one is perfect in this life, 1 John 1:8, makes this perfectly clear. The light of God's purity, shows up any dirt in our lives, God wants us to be rid of it, so that we might be more like Him and our relationship with Him be restored.

Repentance is the natural outcome of God revealing Himself to His people; they must turn from their sin. In revival this repentance produces confession, restitution, reconciliation and many other responses.

Public confession of sin is not pleasant and in certain circumstances can be dangerous for both confessor and hearers, however in revival it just happens as such is the presence of God that scandal is unthinkable and everyone is in the same situation. This is graphically illustrated in the East African Revival from 1935 onwards; one participant described the meetings in this way:

" Missionaries acknowledged as sin their criticism, jealousy, bitterness, resentment, impurity, and anger, lack of vision and love for each other and for those among whom they had come to minister. Africans repented of deep rooted fear, suspicion and mistrust of Europeans, of tribal differences and hatred. As the masks were stripped off and each of us faced the reality of his own sinfulness, there was no need for unhealthy introspection or despair."[31]

Similar stories are told from other great periods of revival. Restitution is another side of repentance in revival. Stolen goods are returned, outstanding debts are paid, employees make good to their employers and vice versa, students turn in awards for cheating in examinations. When God moves the postal services are delighted at the increase in letters, as long outstanding issues are settled by post. Telephones constantly ring as God the Holy Spirit prompts one and another to get in touch over matters from the past. Today the electronic network would come alive

---

31   Bill Butler *Hill Ablaze* P116 Hodder and Stoughton

in revival, just as in the past the same things happened, even though methods were less sophisticated.

One man said this of Duncan Campbell's ministry in the Hebridean Revival:

"Mr. Campbell's ministry cost me a lot, over 10,000 dollars in fact! I had to go back to the United States where I was born and work for a year to make restitution for things I had done as a sinner."[32]

Sadly today as in other ages churches are torn apart by division. Members do not speak to each other, sometimes for years at a time, even families are split apart, and it is an affront to God. In revival as God convicts, so families, friends and churches are put back together again.

Repentance means action, you will never hide revival because its resulting actions are too loud and public.

God is holy and His longing is for His people to be holy. When revival comes, standards change and lives can never be the same again.

These are the main features of revival which in history occur on every occasion when God so works. There are however other features that occur in some revivals but not in others. Whilst this may be difficult to understand, it is good to remember that God is sovereign, it is entirely His prerogative how and when He works. This also should be born in mind with regard to the future, as has been mentioned before, the next revival may be very different from anything in the past or present.

There are four other features that are worth noting in this chapter although there are undoubtedly many others.

---

32   Andrew Woolsey *Duncan Campbell* P164 Hodder and Stoughton

1 - Suffering and Persecution

When God's Spirit stirs His people to move, this invariably causes an opposite stirring which can result in persecution. Revival is costly in many ways, it is no easy answer and certainly its coming will not dispel all our problems, it may even compound them.

It would be true to say that when revival is on the stage, suffering and persecution are often hovering in the wings. Before revival, during revival and after revival there are records of persecution breaking out on God's people sometimes in limited form and other times quite extensively.

Scripture itself seems to indicate that so often God's blessing and suffering go together. Quite naturally Christians desire to know God's blessing and this is absolutely right for them, but to reach that blessing may mean travelling the road of suffering. It is through the times of suffering and hardship that we learn of God in new and deeper ways that will never be found in any other way. Abraham, Job, David, Peter, Paul all learned in this school, as have Christians down through the ages. In revival the blessing of God comes down on His people, but often through the channel of persecution and blessing.

Wesley was dragged from his horse by a baying crowd bent on taking his life. Howell Harris, the Welsh contemporary of Wesley and Whitfield, one of the greatest preachers in Wales who saw in six years a mighty revival that changed the religious and social life of the principality was set upon by a mob and left for dead.

John Foxe in his famous *Book of Martyrs* says:

"The history of Christian martyrdom is in fact the history of Christianity itself, for it is in the arena, at the stake, and in the dungeon that the religion of Christ has won its most glorious triumphs."[33]

It was Bishop Hugh Latimer who said as the flames licked around the martyr's stake in Broad Street, Oxford during the sixteenth century:

"We shall this day light such a candle, by God's grace, in England as I trust shall never be put out."[34]

On 18 March 1496, the godly monk Savonarola who had lashed the evil tyrants of both church and state with his tongue and preaching to crowds of up to six thousand in Florence, preached his last sermon. In less than a month he, along with two compatriots, were hung and burned to death in the Piazza Della Signoria. His sermon concluded with these words:

"I feel myself all burning, all inflamed with the Spirit of the Lord. Oh, Spirit within! You rouse the waves of the sea, as the wind does. You stir the tempest as you pass. I can do no other."[35]

That is the spirit and history of revival.

Not only is it through persecution that Christians suffer in revival, but sometimes the revival is a preparation for what God knows is about to happen to the church. Many revivals have preceded wars and other terrible calamities.

When we pray for revival we need to be aware of what we are praying, it may be that we are with it bringing suffering and persecution to ourselves. Revival is serious business, it is God's business.

---

33   John Foxe *Book of Martyrs*
34   ibid
35   Christopher Hibbert *The Rise and Fall of the House of Medici* P 198 Allen
        Lane

2 - Powerful Preaching

During times of revival God anoints the preaching of His Word in such a way that men and women cannot help but respond to it. Revival sometimes happens as a result of Godly men faithfully preaching but more often at such times preachers are raised up and preaching itself takes a fresh lease of life.

The eighteenth century revival both in the British Isles and America was studded with powerful preaching. In England it was Wesley and Whitfield, in Wales, Howell Harris and Daniel Rowlands whilst in America Jonathan Edwards was preaching in the Spirit's power often accompanied by Whitfield.

The nineteenth century burst forth with a new wave of preaching with the birth of the Primitive Methodist movement. Men such as Hugh Bourne, William Clowes and Billy Bray were preaching to hundreds and setting England ablaze. Charles Finney, Robert Murray McCheyne, Charles Spurgeon, William Booth, to name but a few, all preached in revival with amazing results.

All preaching is dependent upon the work of the Holy Spirit, without it the preaching is empty and the preacher vain. It would seem however that a special unction comes upon the preacher in revival that brings the hearer under deep conviction of sin. Under this anointing from God men and women cannot help but respond to His Word, which produces repentance and changed lives. The Spirit of God cuts deeply into the heart during this preaching and often there are reports of loud cries and groans accompanied with tears during the course of the sermon. Sadly, so much preaching today is "matter of fact", without expecting results, not so in revival for God does the work and the preacher fades into the background.

Duncan Campbell, used of God in the Hebrides is one of the few preachers whose words have been preserved from the midst of revival by means of recording. This is largely due to the fact that revival was scarce in the Western world during the twentieth century. To listen today to this man of God, still stirs the heart and brings tears to the eyes.

By modern standards, Jonathan Edwards would be dismissed in an age of superstars. He would ascend the pulpit steps and taking his notebook in his left hand holding it sometimes no more than six inches from his face and with a candle in the other he would read his sermon. In most Bible Colleges he would be banished from the homiletics class as a non-starter, but thankfully God does not work to our standards. As the message was read in this manner, occasionally with Edwards speaking extemporaneously there was such an anointing from the Holy Spirit that the congregation cried out to God for mercy. Edwards is perhaps most remembered for his sermon entitled "Sinners in the hands of an angry God." It was preached in Enfield, a town in New England and it is reported that so great was the crying at one point, that the preacher's voice was itself drowned and he had to stop and plead for silence to continue. That is Spirit anointed preaching in the midst of revival, so far removed from the preachers who tickle the ears of their listeners with fine words yet without lasting results. When revival came to Enfield under Edwards preaching, the results lasted a lifetime.

Whilst emphasising the place and importance of preaching in revival it must however be said that preaching has not been a prominent feature in every revival. As God swept across America in 1858 it was primarily one large prayer meeting from end to end of the nation with little preaching and no preachers coming to prominence. During the Welsh Revival of 1904/5, Evan Roberts whilst being a great exhorter was not a preacher in the normally understood sense. Often he would walk up and down the church crying just one phrase such as "Bend the church" or similar, this was God's chosen means for that time but not really preaching.

Biblical preaching sets a solid foundation for revival in the Church, when revival comes maybe as a result of that preaching, it will take a new direction under the unique anointing of the Holy Spirit.

3 - Signs and Wonders

When God sends the fire of revival in His people, there is no end to what He may do in their midst. In many times, long before the current interest in the gifts of the Holy Spirit, God has performed mighty wonders in and through His people.

The interesting aspect of these "signs and wonders" in revival is that they usually are an aside and rarely feature prominently in what God is doing. There have been some remarkable accounts of healing during revival on the African continent during the twentieth century. The eye witness accounts of these healings speak of men and women being healed in the course of normal services, often without the preacher being aware, as the presence of God is so real.

It was late in the 1970s, following the reign of terror under Khmer Rouge in Cambodia that God in His wisdom chose to pour out revival blessing in the refugee camps on the border of Thailand. In these conditions of squalor and depravation there was spiritual transformation, many were converted and numerous miracles took place. As one eye witness put it, "no-one sought miracles, they just happened in that atmosphere."

There is evidence of speaking in tongues during the revivals at the beginning of the nineteenth century and again in 1860 as revival broke out in India. There are also accounts of other remarkable happenings in other revivals, although healings and similar signs are rarely mentioned until the twentieth century, when the direction or maybe its sense of priority, seems to change. In England there were healing evangelists such as the Jefferies Brothers and Smith Wigglesworth in the early part of the century, whilst more recent accounts come back from South America, Africa, Indonesia and even China of God's healing power.

The great danger in any generation with signs and wonders is that they can become an end in themselves which totally absorb the life and thinking of the church. It has to be remembered that God reveals something of Himself in revival, which means His holiness will be evident and anything that detracts from that can be a danger however good in itself.

In true revival there is no seeking after spectacular happenings, although that sometimes happens, because people are totally taken over with God! In another account of the East African revival, H.H. Osborn makes this interesting statement:

"In a 'charismatic' understanding of the work of the Holy Spirit, the emphasis seems to be mainly on God bestowing particular spiritual gifts such as 'speaking in tongues', 'prophecy', 'healing', etc. In the experience of those who were first touched by revival in Rwanda and South-West Uganda, these evidences were largely either missing or considered of secondary importance. Their experience of the Holy Spirit led rather to an overwhelming sense of the holiness of God, of the sinfulness of sin, of the effectiveness of the blood of Christ shed on the cross to cleanse from sin, of the assurance of sins forgiven, of the reality of the presence of Christ and of the enabling power of the Holy Spirit to overcome sin."[36]

36   H.H. Osborn *Fire in the Hills*, P 281 Highland Books

In the well documented accounts of Wesley's exploits, there appears to be no recorded incidents of healing, except for the occasion when his horse goes lame and after he prays for it he is able to continue with his journey. Signs and wonders are not evidence in themselves of revival and never have been, but we must however be careful not to limit God. Revival is not about the spectacular, it is about getting right with God.

It may well be that in future revival God will accomplish wonders that human eye has not seen before, that is His privilege, our part is remain open to Him.

4 - God's Use of the Ordinary and Unknown

The last feature of revival I want to mention in this section may be unexpected and some may even feel irrelevant; however in any study of revival it is noticeable that God sometimes chooses to move with unknown men and women, in unusual places and at unexpected times.

When God moves in revival it is not always where men expect it to be or where they want it. He does not always choose the people who are prominent or have position in the church; it is often the ordinary, unlettered person. Sometimes in revival it is not always in the church where we expect it to happen; it maybe that the church is seemingly insignificant or perhaps has different stance to the place where we feel God should work. I remember hearing the Bible Teacher, Judson Cornwall, say, "If you pray for revival, don't be surprised if it breaks out in the church down the road!" It is God's prerogative to work where and when He wills.

A drunken playboy called Howell Harris is converted in 1735; God uses him to touch a spiritually dead Wales. In 1796, a backwood's preacher James McGeady with the care of three small churches in Kentucky directs his people to prayer and within three years there is such an outpouring of God's Spirit that as Edwin Orr records, "intercessors were overtaken by night and day counsel of sinners." No man was more shy than Hugh Bourne who hated the public platform and would never look at his congregation, yet at Mow Cop in Cheshire 1807 he preached to a vast crowd and the power of God came on the people in a way not seen since Wesley and Whitfield.

It was a young man Evan Roberts from the Welsh Valleys who prayed until he had a vision of 100,000 converted in Wales. It was on a Scottish offshore island where revival broke out in 1949, not the mainland of Scotland or England, it was God's choice.

We cannot direct God where and with whom He will work in revival. God's people can only pray that He will so work and be glad when he does, wherever it happens.

Robert Murray McCheyne was a man who saw revival under his ministry in Scotland during the early part of the nineteenth century. He was above all, a man of holiness and humility and that may well account for the reason God was able to use him. In a letter to his friend William Burns, who saw even greater outpourings, he wrote this:

"Be clothed with humility, or you will be a wandering star, for which is reserved the blackness of darkness forever. Let Christ increase; let man decrease. This is my constant prayer for myself and you."[37]

It could well be the case that some of the men and women that we look to and expect to be used in revival are just too big

---

37   Luis Palau *Scottish Fires of Revival* P65-6 D.I.M.E Publications

for God to use. God will not share his glory, in revival it goes only to Him.

As already mentioned there are other features of revival, these are but a few. However prayer, a fear of God, and a conviction of sin and repentance are the expectation for revival. If we expect anything less we deceive ourselves and miss out on God's best.

CHAPTER 5

Revival in the Old Testament

In the previous chapters we have sought to define the term "revival", and looked at some of the features of it. We must now turn to the Scriptures in order to establish a Biblical basis for this study.

In looking at its historical features, the question could legitimately be posed, "Is revival a Biblical concept?". Critics might well argue that revival as we have described it is an invention of Evangelical Christianity which has developed over the past three centuries. It is true that the word "revival" was not used in the sense of describing a religious happening until the year 1702. In that year a spiritual awakening in the church caught the attention of the public at large and it was then referred to as a "revival". Prior to that date the word is not used in this way by those inside or outside of the church.

Although the word "revival" is not used, nevertheless the underlying principles concerning its outworking and overall effect can be seen not only in church history but also as part of the teaching and historical truth of Scripture itself.

There are three main reasons why we should look at this subject from the viewpoint of Scripture.

The first is that every principle and practice exercised by the church must be tested against Scripture. In every generation there have been those led into error because adequate examination has not been given to happenings in the life of the church against Holy Scripture. It is all too easy to accept everything that happens and what we are told without checking the Scriptures for teaching and precedents concerning the issues in hand. If we accept Scripture to be the very Word of God, then it must be our yardstick in all matters pertaining to the church. This must then apply to the subject of revival, otherwise we will never be quite sure whether it is God inspired or man invented, and even with this subject be in danger of error.

The second reason is that many religious groups, particularly those favouring excessive emotional displays and even some who would not hold to true doctrine would claim revival status. If this is the case it is beholden upon us to ensure that when we understand revival it is different from such excesses and that we do not deviate from the truth of Scripture.

The third reason for looking at the subject from Scripture is because we can easily be taken up with books about revival which can become our yardstick rather than the Bible itself. There are numerous fascinating accounts today of revival stories past and present all of which give valuable insight but they are no substitute for the Bible. Let us then turn first of all to the Old Testament to see from where this concept of revival originates.

Revival in the Old Testament

If we look in a Bible Concordance for the word "Revival" we will be frustrated as this actual word does not occur in the Biblical text. The closest word we have to it is the Hebrew word "chayah" (transliterated), which occurs no less than fourteen times in the Old Testament. This word means "to repair, to renew, to restore, to quicken, to make alive". An example of its use is found in Psalm 85:6

"Will you not **revive** us again, that your people may rejoice in you?"

The psalmist here is praying that God will make His people (Israel) alive again towards God. The sin of the people had hindered and gradually killed off their relationship with God so he pleads the case on the basis of God's mercy that it might be revived. The psalmist knows that only after such a revival has taken place will the people's joy be fully restored.

Another example of this is found in Habakkuk's prophecy; Habakkuk 3:2

"Lord, I have heard of your fame; I stand in awe of your deeds. O Lord, renew them in our day, in our time make them known; in wrath remember mercy."

This prophecy is made up of a series of dialogues between the prophet and God. In this section he points back to what God has done in the past with His people and now cries out to God from the depths of his heart that God would perform the same mighty acts in his day and generation. He pleads for God to renew His works, in other words to bring about a state of revival in the nation.

In both of these references, as with others, God is designated as the author of revival and that revival comes to people already in relationship with God.

Although the actual word "revival" does not appear in the Old Testament or for that matter Scripture at all, the concept of revival is made clear throughout.

Principles concerning revival in the Old Testament

The most quoted verse on the subject of revival seems to be in 2 Chronicles 7:14; numerous sermons have been preached from this text stirring God's people to seek His face for revival. It would be true to say that it has been almost overused in this context and sometimes even misused. It is important as with all Scripture, to look both at the preceding and succeeding verses to understand it in its correct context.

"When I shut up the heavens so that there is no rain, or command locusts to devour the land or send plague among my people, if my people, who are called by my name, will humble themselves and pray and seek my face and will turn from their wicked ways, then I will hear from heaven and will forgive their sin and will heal their land. Now my eyes will be open and my eyes attentive to the prayers offered in this place. I have chosen and consecrated this temple so that my Name may be there for ever. My eyes and my heart will always be there."

These are direct words from God to King Solomon following the dedication of the temple in Jerusalem. In the previous chapter he has offered a prayer of dedication to God who responds by sending fire from heaven to consume the burnt offering and the sacrifices and by filling the temple with His glory. The effect of this upon the priests is that they cannot even enter the temple, so real is the presence of God even to perform their priestly functions. The priests are found with the people prostrate before the presence of a Holy God outside of the temple. This incident is very similar to the account we have in Exodus 40 at the setting up of the tabernacle when Moses is prevented from entering the sanctuary because of the glory of the Lord.

Both of these accounts illustrate what happens at a time of revival. God comes to His people from heaven and there is such a sense of God's holiness because of His presence that men and women are prostrate before Him.

It is after this demonstration from God that now in verse

seven God speaks directly to Solomon. With the backdrop of what has already happened and knowing the backsliding nature of His people, God makes this promise. It is as if God is saying, "I just know how you as a people will be when all this euphoria wears off, but I am willing to come to you again as I did at the dedication of the temple".

God makes His position very clear, when the people backslide and turn from His ways it will result in disaster coming to the nation. It may come in the form of drought, or devastation from locusts or even physical plague on the people. This is the judgement of God upon them, whatever form it takes, and it is the direct result of their own behaviour. When this happens, (and the assumption is from this that it will happen), God promises to bring revival to His people if they return to Him in obedience. God requires then from His people three actions: 1) humility – "humble obedience", 2) a return to prayer – "pray and seek my face", 3) repentance - "turn from their wicked ways".

The promise God makes to His people if they respond in this way, is that He will hear their prayers from Heaven itself and come down again to heal their land.

This then is a promise and picture of revival, given directly to King Solomon for God's people Israel following the construction and dedication of the temple. It was God's promise for His people under the Old Covenant and we shall see that it was worked out in practice on many occasions.

A Picture of Revival

In Isaiah's prophecy, we are given a marvellous description of what happens in revival (Isaiah 64:1-4). Here in the final part of his prophecy, Isaiah prays to God that He will once again show

His hand in power, just as had been promised to Solomon in time past.

"Oh that you would rend the heavens and come down, that the mountains would tremble before you! As when fire sets twigs ablaze and causes water to boil, come down and make your name known to your enemies and cause the nations to quake before you! For when you did awesome things we did not expect, you came down, and the mountains trembled before you. Since ancient times no-one has heard, no ear has perceived, no eye has seen any God besides you, who acts on behalf of those who wait for Him."

The prophet's prayer is that God would come down and meet His people at their time of need. This then is a definition of revival, "God coming down". Revival always starts with God when man can do nothing for himself.

What happens then when God comes down to His people? The picture that Isaiah describes is one familiar to geologists and observers of geographical events across the world. It is like the action of a volcano which very often has been graphically captured for us by television cameras.

When the volcano erupts, molten lava is sent cascading down the side of the mountain which sweeps all before it. Trees and bushes are consumed in the fire, massive rocks and even houses are pushed to one side like children's toys. As it meets with the streams and rivers in its course, and eventually the sea itself, so water is brought to the boil like a steaming cauldron. In the same way when God comes to His people everything is swept aside at His presence. Divisions of generations, gossip and slander, every kind of malpractice, in fact all sin in God's people is exposed by the consuming fire of His presence.

In this prayer Isaiah also reveals what happens as a result of God visiting His people. It is that God's name may be made known among the nations. The effect is twofold, (1) as God's people are so thrilled with their experience of Him they take His word to other peoples, and (2) as the nations around observe what is happening they are left in no doubt as to the validity of the Living God.

This description of revival as given by Isaiah has been experienced by God's people down through the ages in one way or another. In one sense it could be said that this is what happened on the day of Pentecost, God's presence first coming down on the disciples and then to the crowds gathered from many nations. Gilbert Egerton quotes such incidents in revival:

" The remarkable sense of God may pervade a building, a community or a district, and those who come within its range are profoundly affected. At the beginning of the 1904 Awakening in Wales, a revival meeting was in progress throughout the night near the town of Gorseinon. A notorious careless and sinful miner returning from his shift at 4 AM saw the light in the chapel and went to investigate. As soon as he opened the chapel door, he was immediately overwhelmed by a sense of God's presence and exclaimed, "Oh God is here!" He was afraid to enter the building or depart, and there on the door step where he stood, a saving work of grace began in his soul. Similar stories could be told of the 1858 American Revival. As ships drew near American ports, they came within a "zone of heavenly influence". Sudden conviction and conversion were a common occurrence on board ship – In one ship a captain and the entire crew of thirty men found Christ at sea and entered the harbour rejoicing.[38]

In more recent times missionaries have recounted of how in Argentina when God was working powerfully in one church, young men stood outside mocking what was happening. One of them was dared to enter the building and immediately he crossed the threshold he was struck down under conviction of sin.

Cyclical Renewal in the Old Testament

When we look at the history of the Children of Israel in the Old Testament a definite pattern emerges in their spiritual life as a nation. It is best described as one of "cyclical renewal". It happens when complacency sets in and they forget all that God has done for them as a nation in the past. Their complacency leads to sin, their sin brings upon them the judgement of God (this may be in the form of invasion by enemies, plagues or pestilence), in desperation they then seek God and out of His mercy He sends deliverance. The hallmarks of revival are in this pattern, as it is when they are at their lowest ebb, they seek God (prayer), they turn to Him in repentance and there is a sense of His presence as God is once again put first in the life of the nation.

The book of Judges demonstrates this series of cycles where we see God raising up men and women Like Gideon, Samson and Deborah to deliver Israel in their time of need. The interesting factor of these revivals is that the effect usually lasts for just one generation and then the slide downwards starts again.

In examining the history of both Israel and the Church it seems that God's people fall into the same pattern of spiritual life in every generation. What can be seen from the history of Israel before Christ, can also be seen in the history of the Church after Christ. We forget all too easily and too quickly what God has accomplished for us in the past and allow our human nature to dominate the present. It is for this reason revival is necessary for this and every generation, whilst we can learn from the past we must never rely upon it.

There are many such examples of revival in the Old Testament record and we shall now look at some of the major incidents.

Examples of Revival in the Old Testament

Judges 2. On this occasion it is an angel of the Lord who brings a cutting message from God to His people. In spite of all God has done for them in the past they have been guilty of disobedience to God's commands (verse 2) so God tells them that their enemies will be a stumbling block to them. As a result of God's direct word to them, they respond with repentance and weeping so much so that the very place where this happens is called Bokim which means "weepers". In this account there is no record of the overwhelming presence of God coming upon the people but there is certainly a return to right relationship with God through the sacrifices.'

1 Samuel 7. This time of revival occurred when Israel as a nation had become both morally and spiritually bankrupt. This once great nation, with all its past blessings and inheritance was now spiritually dying upon its feet. Those who were leaders and should have been setting an example to the people were themselves guilty of gross sin against God (2:16-17 &29). Their immoral lifestyle was a common fact among the people (2:22), it seems that the nation had at this time reached the lowest depths. It is no wonder that in those conditions God's word was not heard by the leaders or the people (3:1).

It is at such times that God has graciously visited his people in revival power, both with Israel and with the church. When all around is darkness and there is no light from within, revival then is the only answer. Church history shows us that revival comes to a dying church in a decadent society. The picture could not have been worse for Israel, they appeared to be all but finished as God's people, but there are no conditions beyond the reach of God. D.M.Panton writes this:

"It is a foolish blunder to suppose that any age can be too evil for revival" [39]

In chapter seven we have the account of the actual revival when God speaks to the people through his prophet Samuel. The message is very clear (verse3) to return wholeheartedly to God and put away every semblance of evil from their midst, the result of this is (verse 4-6) repentance and confession of their sin. This gives to them a new confidence and dependence upon God (verse 8) and God hears their prayers, comes down and joins them in battle against the Philistines and they enjoy a glorious victory (verse 9-11). God has now become the central focus point for them as they give to Him the glory (verse 12).

This account is a beautiful example of revival and Ted S. Rendall of the Prairie Bible Institute commenting on it says:

"When God is at work, then we may expect the unusual; we may see the 'impossible'; we may share in the new thing of God's grace. Problems that have defied solution for years are resolved; situations that have resisted change are transformed; tensions that have built up over a period of time are eased. Despair gives way to hope, pessimism gives way to a glorious optimism in the Lord, fear gives way to courage and confidence in the Lord."[40]

1 Kings 18: This is perhaps the most well-known incident in the life of the prophet Elijah, his conflict with the prophets of Baal on Mount Carmel. Once again at a time of national crisis, when the nation is in the grip of evil powers, God raises up His man for the moment; Elijah. As the forces of evil are challenged and Elijah calls upon God so the fire from heaven falls (verse38). The result is that in the presence of God the people are prostrated before

---

39   Ted S. Randall *Fire in the Church* P16 Moody Press
40   ibid

Him and there is recognition of the power and majesty of God.

1 Chronicles 29. After a disastrous period with a series of evil kings on the throne of Judah, now Hezekiah becomes king at the age of twenty-five. He was very different to his immediate predecessors as we are told (verse 2): *"He did what was right in the eyes of the Lord"*.

Immediately as he commences his reign he sets about to clean out the evil that was infecting the nation. He seeks God's face for the nation (verse10) in accordance with the promise given to his forefather Solomon (2 Chron. 7:14). The result is that first of all the purge starts with the house of God and then the people as a whole are called to return to God (30:6-9). As the leaders and people alike return so God is faithful to His word (30:20) and heals the nation bringing about a time of great rejoicing.

Other examples of revival can be seen with the return to Jerusalem from Babylon as recorded in both Ezra and Nehemiah. There is also an interesting account of revival in the story of the prophet Jonah where there is repentance and turning to God by the people of Nineveh following the proclamations from the reluctant Jonah. In this case it is not God's people who experience God's mercy but a heathen nation. This may have been long term for the benefit of God's people, but such is His mercy and sovereignty that the revival experience can come to the most unexpected places and people.

In Habakkuk chapter three the prophet gives a graphic description of the power of God and pleads for that power to come again as an awakening in his time. There are other accounts of revival/awakenings worthy of mention:

Judges 7 (Gideon)
2 Chron. 15:1-15) (Asa)
2 Kings 11&12, 2 Chron. 23&24 (Joash)
2Kings 22&23, 2 Chron.34&35 (Josiah)

Dr. Wilbur Smith notes nine characteristics of revival in the Old Testament:

"They occurred in a day of deep moral darkness and national depression.

They began in the heart of one consecrated servant of God who became the energising power behind it, the agent used by God to quicken and lead the nation back in faith and obedience to Him.

Each revival rested on the Word of God and most were the result of preaching and proclaiming God's laws with power.
All resulted in a return to the worship of Jehovah.
Each witnessed destruction of idols where they existed.
In each revival, there was a recorded separation from sin.
In every revival there was a return to blood sacrifices.
Almost all recorded revivals show a restoration of great joy and gladness'
Each revival was followed by a period of great national prosperity."[41]

Revival clearly is a theme running right through Scripture; the nature of God's people makes it a necessity. The Old Testament contains an historical account of revival, revealing a numbers of principles and promises concerning it, but above all it demonstrates the mercy of God in sending revival time and time again.

---

41   Fischer Reviving Revivals P63-4 (quoted by W. Pratney Revival P20-1
        Whitaker Press

CHAPTER 6

Revival in the New Testament

We now turn from the Old Testament, having looked at the case for revival with the Children of Israel, to the New Testament and the church age. The question we now need to be asking is, if Israel was subject to a pattern of continuous renewal in its spiritual life, should the church expect that same pattern? After all one can argue that Israel was under the Old Covenant which surely means that the old way of life has passed away.

Jeremiah (Jeremiah 31:31-34) speaks about the Old Covenant being replaced by something completely new. He speaks about the Old Covenant (31:32) being constantly broken although God showed them all the love and care of a faithful husband. God never broke the covenant, it was His people who were unable to make it work which caused this cycle of renewal which is particularly seen in the book of Judges.

It is Jesus Himself who ushers in the New Covenant (Luke 22:20) as He takes the cup of wine with His disciples on the Last Supper. The New Covenant that He establishes is totally workable as it does not rely upon continual sacrifices for sin, but on a once for all sacrifice made with His blood. Those then who have experienced the new birth (John 3:3) and come to faith in Christ through the merits of His shed blood are therefore under this New Covenant. Every member of the church is under the New Covenant, it is the New Covenant age.

If this is the case, should then the church be subject to cyclical renewal or should it enjoy continuous revival?

Richard Lovelace in *Dynamics of Spiritual Life* makes this helpful observation:

"Why don't the cycles end now, as God's people are led into a steady conquest of the occupying power? After all, 'the reason the Son of God appeared was to destroy the works of the devil' (1 John 3:8). Jesus told His disciples, ' Behold, I have given you authority to tread upon serpents and scorpions, and over all the power of the enemy; and nothing shall hurt you' (Luke 10:19). In the atonement, He disarmed the principalities and powers and made public example of them, triumphing over them' (Col. 2:15). Paul assured the Romans that 'the God of peace will soon crush Satan under your feet' (Romans 16:20). So it seems at first that this victory ought to be constant and that the cyclical model of spiritual renewal under the Old Covenant should be replaced by a model of continuous renewal under the Lordship of Christ. But even under the New Covenant, with an eternal and infinitely perfect leader, the people of God cannot expect to prevail unless they follow that leader." [42]

Revival in the New Testament

As in the Old Testament the actual word revival or revive in the sense of our understanding does not appear. The nearest equivalent word is found in 2 Timothy 1:6 where Paul urges Timothy to "fan the flame", or stir up the gift within him. It is in fact a call to revive, but this is not a reference to revival.

The other two references where this occurs are in Romans 7:9 & 14:9, again it is used in a different sense, once in reference to sin and the other to the resurrection.

In the record of the church as we have it in both Acts and

42   Richard Lovelace *Dynamics of Spiritual Life* P73 IVP

the epistles, revival is not a word that is used or known. The reason for this is that the church was something completely new. That which had been promised by the Old Testament prophets, the outpouring of the Holy Spirit had now taken place. The incredible events that took place on the Day of Pentecost as recorded in Acts 2 were not a reviving of something old but a new age being established under the New Covenant. However the life and witness of this new born church hold all the marks of God's outpourings on the church in other generations that we refer to as revival.

Let us look at the events on the Day of Pentecost to see how many of the features normally associated with revival (as mentioned previously) actually occur.

Prayer – After the ascension of Jesus to Heaven (Acts 1:9-11), the disciples return to Jerusalem where they wait as Jesus had instructed them, to receive the promised Holy Spirit. One hundred and twenty were there including His immediate disciples along with His mother and brothers. They meet in an upper room just as they had for the Passover and their time is spent in constant prayer (1:14)

The prayer meeting lasts until the Day of Pentecost when the Holy Spirit comes upon them in a "volcano" like eruption, with the sound of a gale force wind filling the house, the appearance of what seemed like flames of fire over each one of them and they began to speak in new languages.

This outpouring of the Holy Spirit was born with the labour pains of prayer. In the midst of confusion and fear they remained obedient and resolute, praying until the promise of God was fulfilled before their very eyes.

It was not only born out of prayer but prayer continued

after the day of Pentecost. As three thousand were swept into the church that day, so this young church continued in prayer (1:42). It is no wonder that the mighty moving of the Holy Spirit continued with such a force of prayer warriors.

One of the essential features of revival is prayer; the day of Pentecost was no exception.

The Fear of God – The happenings on that day were so dramatic they certainly brought about a reaction of amazement (1:6-12) to the many Jews in Jerusalem for the Feast. To the disciples it was evident that this was what had been promised and now they were experiencing a touch of the presence of God. A mixture of fear and mockery ran through the crowd, reactions not uncommon when God reveals Himself to His people. It is with these events in the forefront of everyone's mind that Peter stands up and preaches the most famous sermon in history.

The response from the people seems to come almost before he has finished speaking (1:37), they are overwhelmed at the presence of God and challenged by Peter's cutting words that they cry out asking "What shall we do?"

It is quite evident that on the Day of Pentecost and during the weeks that followed there was an extraordinary sense of God's presence with His people which resulted in some dramatic experiences. Such has been the case at other times of revival.

A Conviction of sin – The presence and power of God always brings about a conviction of sin as men and women realise their state before a Holy God. As these people cry out under such conviction, Peter's first response to them was "repent", (2:38). The account of Peter's message is in an abbreviated form in Acts 2, but the thrust of it is quite clear (2:40) to turn away from their sin and the corruption of their generation.

Three thousand responded to this cutting message and whenever God has visited His people in revival, one of the first results has been repentance either from the preaching or directly from the sense of God's presence.

Suffering and persecution – On the Day of Pentecost itself, as the disciples gave expression to what they were experiencing; there was initial persecution, (2:13) with a storm of ribald laughter and mockery raining upon them from confused onlookers. However within days the leaders of the church, Peter and John are thrown into prison and brought before the Jewish rulers (4:3) following the miraculous healing of a crippled man.

Through two thousand years of church history, persecution has trailed the church like a dog following its master. It is there at the birth of the church and has continued in every generation and culture where Christianity has left its mark. When the blessing of God comes upon the church such persecution is not withdrawn, often by virtue of what is happening to God's people, it intensifies.

Mighty preaching – What has happened? The fisherman from Galilee who just a few weeks previous was denying to a servant girl his association with Jesus is now standing before a massive crowd confidently addressing them. Yes, it is the same Peter, transformed by the power of the Holy Spirit preaching with the same authority as the prophets in the Old Testament and John the Baptist.

His message is simple yet direct, taking the Old Testament scriptures and explaining them in the light of events now taking place. The effect of this preaching is that his Jewish hearers from all over the Mediterranean area are so challenged they respond even before he has finished speaking. With such preaching there is no need for the completion of decision cards or expensive counselling or follow up procedures (which sometimes have their place), the response is immediate and genuine because God has done His work.

As we follow through in the Acts, the history of the church in the atmosphere of revival; we see not only Peter but Philip, Stephen, Paul and Barnabas all preaching with great power with results following. In the church there have always been great preachers but it is in revival that it is more prominent and most effective.

Signs and wonders – Acts 2:43 makes it clear that various miraculous signs were done through the apostles and witnessed by many. The next chapter gives us an example of one such miracle (3:7) when a middle aged man, crippled from birth is instantly healed. As with the preaching so miracles continue to happen during the Acts "revival".

Signs and wonders are no guarantee of revival and often such manifestations do not occur in revival but we should never be surprised at what God may accomplish at such times.

Use of the ordinary – No-one could have been more ordinary than Peter. Other disciples like Matthew would have been better educated and probably far more articulate than Peter, but the Holy Spirit chose to use him. Peter was used to a rugged way of life and far more at home with his boat and nets than standing before a crowd. He could use his tongue but it was usually in the wrong place; on one occasion, Jesus when Peter had spoken is forced to publicly rebuke him (Mark 14:66-72), and again during the trial of Jesus, Peter reverts back to the uncouth swear words of a northern fisherman, yet it is through Peter that God chooses to speak on the Day of Pentecost.

The church in its birth had every sign of revival (and probably others not recorded) and according to the Acts it largely seemed to live in the good of it. The results were quite spectacular, the cost to the church was very great and whilst there were mistakes and problems, revivals in subsequent generations have usually been only a shadow of that period.

To live in revival was the norm for the early church and under the New Covenant the possibility of continuing in this way is there, whilst the church keeps close to its Master. The problem is that being the human creatures we are, we become so easily distracted by the desires of the flesh, the subtlety of sin and the devil himself, so much so that we end up in as bad a state (and sometimes worse) than the Children of Israel under the Old Covenant. Revival means the church returning to that which it is meant to be, in other words becoming like and experiencing the same as in the Acts.

Dr. Martyn Lloyd-Jones in one of his inspiring sermons on revival says this:

"Any reading of church history, even that which is cursory and superficial, will; I think, bring out this principle abundantly clearly – that every time you get one of these great, and glorious and mighty periods, you will find that in every instance it seems to be returning to something that had obtained before. Indeed, I will go further – you will find that every one of them seems to be returning to what you can read in the book of Acts of the Apostles." [43]

---

43   Martyn Lloyd –Jones *Revival, can we make it happen?* P27-8 Marshall-
          Pickering

Warnings and Promises to the Church

The account we have of the early church in the Acts is to say the very least a story of success. Whilst Dr. Luke, the author, does not minimise the faults, he has to record an account of amazing events. It starts with a handful of bewildered men and women who seem to be lost without their leader and within an incredible short period of time they are themselves leading a church numbering thousands. Like a forest fire spreading through the tinder dry foliage, so this church grows both numerically and in maturity. It starts in the main city of a Mediterranean state under the occupation of the largest and harshest dictatorship known to the world and with the most limited forms of communication spreads to touch every corner of that empire. This is revival at its height and with it has come every blessing, surprises and hardship that might be expected when God graciously comes down on the people.

Success story as it is however; it only covers a relatively short period of time, probably no more than thirty years (Ad 31-60). The chilling reality is that by the time the letters in our New Testament were written by Paul and others, many problems and errors had crept into the church and the first zeal and love was no longer there. It is for this very reason that letters like Corinthians and Galatians were written in the first place.

It seems like their forefathers in the Old Testament, the flame of the initial glory had burned very low and was now little more than a smouldering ember.

It is a sad fact that when we come to the last book in our New Testament, the Revelation to the Apostle John, we find Jesus Himself coming into the picture and addressing His church in most severe tones. In Revelation chapters 1-3 we have the last recorded words of Jesus directed to the church. It is important therefore to hear them, to see how Jesus Himself assesses the church.

Most scholars agree that the Revelation was given to John whilst exiled on the island of Patmos during the last decade of the first century. The church by this time had undergone perhaps its most devastating era of persecution while Nero was emperor in Rome; many had been slaughtered by hideous means devised to please the bloodthirsty Roman citizens and their rulers. The despotic Nero himself had enjoyed the spectacle of seeing Christians crucified in his own garden and having them set alight by fire in order to provide light on the drunken orgies for his friends. This persecution however had only served to strengthen the church and incredibly encouraged others to join their ranks. The problems that the church faced at this time were not from persecution without but from division and error within. What Nero was unable to destroy, the church members very nearly did themselves.

Every conceivable corruption, both morally and spiritually was there in the church at the end of the first century, what a sorry state it looked! This is why Jesus steps into the scene through the vision given to John and addresses the churches. The messages that He brings are addressed quite specifically to individual churches in Asia Minor but they are nevertheless representative of the church as a whole both then and now.

In an area that is today part of modern Turkey, these seven churches each very different yet each one known to each other through the effective system of communication developed by the Roman Empire, all have problems, some of which threaten their very existence. To five of the seven churches Jesus has to bring a strong message of condemnation, the language He uses is sometimes surprising but this only serves to emphasise the serious nature of the situation. It is however important to realise why Jesus does this; he is not being judgmental or allowing His anger at their behaviour to overflow, but He is addressing them, out of love, it is because He loves the church and He does not want to lose any part of it and wants it to enjoy the benefits of living in close relationship with Him. Let us now take a brief tour around the churches and hear the message that Jesus brings to each.

Ephesus Rev. 2:1-7

This was a church in one of the great cities of the Roman Empire, also one of the great religious centres. Numerous gods were worshipped here but all were overshadowed by the Temple of Diana which dominated the city. This was pagan religion at its worst with sorcery and prostitution being at its heart.

Paul realised the significance of the place, which is why he spent two years seeing the church established and built up. It had so much to commend it, which must have warmed the heart of John who it is alleged spent his last years there. It was hardworking (v.2), it took a strong stand against evil (v.2), it safeguarded the truth (v.2), but Jesus says they have forsaken their first love (v.4)

Once their love for Jesus was so strong and real, now it was merely a matter of words. Jesus in fact likens their relationship to that which happens in divorce, which was once warm, is now cold. The direction therefore that he gives is REPENT and become as you were at first.

Smyrna Rev. 2:8-11

The message to Smyrna is very different, it is one of encouragement. Here was a church that was poor because of its stand against the bribery and corruption of the business world by refusing to acknowledge the lordship of Caesar, as was required by all who wanted to trade. They were effectively prevented from making a living in the normal way which resulted in wholesale poverty among the membership. Already persecution had come to this church and more was yet to come; so the word of Jesus to them is BE FAITHFUL, even to the point of death.

Pergamum Rev. 2:12-17

Pergamum was an evil place, with every kind of immorality and deviation being practised within its walls. Jesus sees it as a place where Satan is at its very heart (v.13), yet in spite of all that was happening around them the church as a whole had remained faithful and some had even endured a martyr's death (v.13). There were however those who had been led astray to compromise and corruption, in that same way as Balaam (Numbers 22-24) had led the Children of Israel astray from God's ways. To those who have fallen in this way, Jesus calls them to REPENT, otherwise judgment will follow.

Thyatira Rev. 2:18-29

This city was not significant in a political or historical sense but was however an important place for trade. It was ideally situated due to the roads going through the centre of the city, rather like modern cities such as Birmingham and Bristol at the hub of a motorway network. Every type of trade flourished there which resulted in the emergence of numerous trade guilds.

There were goldsmiths, silversmiths, leatherworkers, tailors, woodworkers and every trade known to the world at that time, each represented by its own guild. In order to be a member of one of these guilds it required initiation ceremonies often involving sexual rites which as with Smyrna, prevented Christians from joining and thus being able to trade.

Again it was hard to be a Christian in this city, and Jesus has much to commend them for (v.19), but what had happened was that they had allowed an immoral woman who Jesus refers to as Jezebel to infiltrate their ranks and trap some of the church leaders into immorality themselves. It seems almost ironic that having made such a stand against the evil in the trade guilds that one wicked woman is now able to lead them astray. Jesus says to this church that because they have tolerated evil in their midst, they must REPENT otherwise judgment will come to them.

Sardis Revelation 3:1-6

Sardis was a proud city living on its reputation from the past. It was a place of seeming security due to its geographical position which caused its people to become quite complacent. This very complacency had in fact caused the defeat of the city in its past history. Complacency can be infectious and the Christians had been so infected that when Jesus looks at them He sees them as good as dead, (3:1). The message to this church is therefore to wake up from the state of deadness and REPENT.

Philadelphia Revelation 3:7-13

No harsh words are directed to the church at Philadelphia, this is one of the messages of encouragement. A church that has been faithful and although seen by many to be weak, is seen by Jesus as strong. They are told to hold on and not waver even though trials and persecution may come their way.

Laodicea Revelation 3:14-22

This is probably the best known of both the churches and the letters, many sermons have been preached from this passage of Scripture. It is however perhaps the saddest letter of them all as Jesus looks at the church And sees that it is neither "hot nor cold" (v.15). Outside the city gate was a water fountain, it contained spa water which had travelled some six miles from neighbouring Hierapolis and although it had left there piping hot it was now only lukewarm. Jesus says to those Christians that they are just like the water outside their gates and they have the same affect upon Him as lukewarm spa water can have, they make Him feel sick.

It is a sobering message but Jesus still loves the church (v.19) and He wants it to come back to what it should be, so again His word is REPENT. There is a beautiful promise with this letter in verse 20 which is one of the best known verses in the New Testament. The promise is that He is waiting for them to return in repentance and longing for them to invite Him back so that fellowship may be restored. No church could have drifted farther away than Laodicea but there is hope as Jesus promises to in effect "revive them" if they repent.

The conclusion from these letters to the Asia Minor churches is that Jesus loves the church in spite of what it has become. He is grieved as He sees the state of the church and it causes Him great pain to see it in such a state. In order that the church might be revived He requires in each case the church to repent. This has been the road to revival in both Old and New Testament eras and whilst revival is always a sovereign act of God, the Risen Lord, because of His love for the church can only but respond when He sees genuine RENPENTANCE.

In 1904 the prayer of God's servant Evan Roberts was "Bend the Church and save the world"; and as repentance came to the church in Wales so with it came an avalanche of blessing sweeping 100,000 souls into the Kingdom in a matter of just a few months.

It was the same for the Moravian revival of 1725 onwards, which we have previously mentioned:

"The refugees on Count Nicolaus Zinzendorf's German estates were Protestants of various persuasions. Their never ending disputes finally impelled Zinzendorf to a full-time ministry of reconciliation and prayer as a last resort.

On the twelfth of May 1727, the whole group of settlers promised to bury their differences and to live in peace. As a result, there came a wonderful effusion of the Spirit. In late July, certain brethren decided to maintain a watch of prayer at a hill near Herrhut; the striking verses of the first epistle of John were their reading. On August 10, the pastor of the congregation at Bethelsdorf was overcome with conviction, and he and his people continued in prayer and singing and supplication and weeping till midnight. Another Pentecost had begun, with like results in their spiritual transformation and their exertions in carrying the gospel to the ends of the earth. Through this Moravian revival, German Pietism affected both the Evangelical Revival in Britain and the great Awakening in the American colonies." [44]

As with Israel in the Old Testament so with the church in the New Testament there is God ordained order that prayer for revival will result in conviction of sin and repentance, and repentance results in prayer for revival. The two are indivisible, but necessary for the church in every generation.

---

44   J. Edwin Orr *The restudy of Revival and Revivalism* 1981

CHAPTER 7

Results of Revival

As we have considered in previous chapters, when revival comes it is primarily for the benefit and blessing of God's people in bringing them back to a right relationship with Him. Historical records however show that when it happens, numerous aspects of life, both in the church and the community are affected. Some would see this as the prime reason for desiring revival, in itself this may be most commendable but these results in whatever form they come are only a bi-product from what God has done directly with His people. Revival brings back God's order in the lives of His people and this spills over into the society at large. Revival does change a community or a nation, but only as God has first brought change in His people's hearts.

It is therefore important to realise the purpose of revival when looking at the results, otherwise the results however good may become the end in itself.

At the beginning of the eighteenth century, England was in a state of moral and spiritual darkness. We may look at the situation in our generation and think it to be bad but it is no more and probably less than was faced at that time.

Drunkenness flourished with both the poor who drank to blot out their miserable existence, and the rich who had nothing better to do. Dallimore in his account of the life of George Whitfield tells of how gin flowed freely in the streets, especially in large cities like London. Every sixth house in the capital was purported to be a gin shop, the notice commonly hung outside such establishments would read: "Drunk for a penny, dead drunk tuppence, free straw." Hogarth, the famous artist, depicted scenes in his cartoons of London streets with mothers lying drunk in the gutter while their children starved.

Crime was commonplace with highwaymen and smugglers plying their "trades" all over the country, often with violence. Petty thieving was at epidemic proportions largely caused through the vast inequality between rich and poor. Over six hundred crimes carried the death penalty which was death by hanging and this in itself became a daily form of entertainment for the masses outside the prisons each morning.

The established church at the beginning of the eighteenth century was in a deplorable state.

"Lambeth Palace had its balls and routs; music parties for Sunday evenings even the bishops countenanced, and card parties were not infrequent on the Sabbath evening. The humbler classes imitated their betters, a sneer at religion was wit; the parson was the standing joke, and the Church was used chiefly to rail at...millions had never heard a sermon!" [45]

Morality and standards in public life were at an all-time low, corruption was a common occurrence and it was estimated that as few as six of the members of parliament actually attended church. The theatre was crude and vulgar; cock fighting and other forms of brutal sport were the regular and popular sources of entertainment. Above all the church seemed impotent with its bishops and clergy corrupt and immoral like their counterparts in parliament.

England was heading for disaster; it was caught up in a landslide of evil with seemingly nothing to halt the impeding

---

45   A. Seymour *The Life and Times of Selina Countess of Huntingdon* Tentmaker 2000 vol.2 P618-9

destruction and nobody caring about it. Then on 24 May 1738 at a Moravian meeting house in Aldersgate, London, John and Charles Wesley were converted, that was God's turning point. When the nation faced disintegration, God stepped in and through these two men and others, brought about the greatest revival ever witnessed on the British Isles.

Secular historians cautiously record that England was saved from a fate such as befell France in the French Revolution through the Great Awakening. In France the peasants turned to atheism, in England they turned to God's Word.

The events of the eighteenth century may be explained in the light of political or social action but few would deny that these largely came about due to the upturn in the spiritual temperature of the nation. Such is the effect of revival, turning about nations and changing the people's standards.

We shall now take a look at some of the results or bi-products of revival.

Society is Changed

Revival to the lifeless church often comes, as in Wesley's day, when society itself is at a low ebb, both morally and spiritually. In one sense this is hardly surprising if the church is meant to be light and salt in society and it is not fulfilling its task, after all who else is able to do it? So when the church is changed by its restored relationship to Jesus it begins to move out into society and accomplish the task for which it was chosen, reaching the lost and changing society.

Taking a look at some of the great revivals let us see ways in which society was so changed.

Crime reduced

During the revival of 1859 and in the years following it was noted in Ireland that crime was greatly reduced. In Ulster judges found themselves at times redundant as there were no cases to bring before them and at one time police recorded there were actually no prisoners in the cells. The police were delighted by the effects of the revival, their workload being considerably lessened. One courtroom in Anglesey is reported to have erupted into hymn singing in Welsh.

The Times newspaper on 7 March 1905 reported:
"During the six months before the revival began, the number of people summoned at Bridgend Police Court from Llynffi Valley numbered 700, but the average since the revival movement spread there has been not more than 2 per week." [46]

Who does not want to see crime reduced? Politicians, police, and social workers constantly fight in what seems to be a losing battle, yet when God moves in revival victory, it can occur overnight. Most revivals can give account of such occurrences, surely then revival is good for society!

Drunkenness reduced.

Drunkenness and its attendant problems have always faced society and they are only amplified when it has become materialistic and self-centred. When revival comes men and women are so changed that they no longer need to be reliant on alcohol. This is borne out in many of the periods of revival both in the British Isles and in other countries.

---

46   *The Times* 7 March 1905

The easy availability of gin which started back in 1689 made drunkenness an all too common problem in the eighteenth century during the time of Wesley and Whitfield. As lives were transformed through their preaching of the Gospel so many were released from the slavery of alcohol. In writing to the Bishop of London in 1747 concerning the effect of his preaching, Wesley says:

"The habitual drunkard that was, is now temperate in all things. The whoremonger now flees fornication. He that stole steals no more, but works with his hands. He that cursed or swore, perhaps in every sentence, has now learned to serve the Lord with fear and rejoice unto Him with reverence. Those formerly enslaved to various habits of sin are now brought to uniform habits of holiness. These are demonstrable facts. I can name the men, with their home addresses."[47]

One of the results of the 1859 revival in Ulster was the closing of McKenzie's whiskey distillery in Belfast which up to that time was producing 1,200,000 gallons per year. Public houses were forced to close their doors and a report in the *Belfast Newsletter* on the revival states that "whiskey drinking had been greatly reduced." One of the publicans was converted and he ultimately became a leading minister of the Gospel.

It was claimed that during the three months of the revival in Wales of 1904/5 more was accomplished to sober up the country than the previous efforts of the temperance movement of many years.

I can personally remember stories being told by Duncan Campbell concerning the revival in the Hebrides where he related that drinking houses across the island had been closed.

---

47   John Wesley *The Nature of Revival* P 217/8 Edited by C.G.Weakley, Bethany House Publishers

Immorality, injustice, gambling, corruption, violence along with so many other evils are cleansed away in the flood that flows from revival. One of the more unusual results of revival was found in Wales in 1905. Vast numbers of the mining community were converted, men who had been drunkards and blasphemers were transformed overnight. Chaos for some while then ensued in the mines as the pit ponies refused to work because they no longer understood the commands from these men. Previously they had responded to cursing and swearing, but now the men's language was clean and wholesome and as far as the poor ponies were concerned it might just as well have been in Chinese! This could only have been a temporary setback for the mine owners themselves reported a considerably increased output during and following the revival. Texts were chalked on the mine shaft walls and many a prayer meeting took place in those underground tunnels.

Revival may well be for God's people but its benefit to society as a whole is immeasurable.

Social Reform takes place

In looking at history it is interesting to note just how many social reforms have taken place as a result of revival, either directly or indirectly. In the same way as when a great ship goes to sea leaving behind it a wake, so revival leaves a host of new agencies and societies involved in various avenues of social action. Such organisations as Dr.Barnados, the Y.M.C.A, the Salvation Army and many others can all trace their origins to a period of revival.

The abolition of the slave trade was brought about through pressure placed upon politicians by Christians in revival. John Wesley was deeply concerned about this vile trade that was rooted into the social and economic life of England. He in fact wrote a paper entitled: *"Thoughts Upon Slavery"*, which was a direct attack on this trade which he had encountered as such a strong force in cities like Bristol. At the very end of his life he was corresponding with William Wilberforce, urging him to take the fight through parliament and not to rest until this offence against the nation was obliterated. A facsimile of his letter can be read today in Wesley's original chapel, The New Room in Bristol.

Charles Finney (1792-1875), a man who God used remarkably in revival during the nineteenth century in America and whose famous lectures on revival have been a text for students of the subject to study ever since was extremely concerned about social reform, especially on the issue of slavery. He became an active abolitionist, even refusing to allow those who owned slaves to participate in communion. As a pastor in New York he made this statement:

"When I first went to New York, I had made up my mind on the question of slavery, and was exceedingly anxious to arouse public attention to the subject. I did not, however, turn aside to make it a hobby, or divert the attention of the people from the work of converting souls. Nevertheless, in my prayers and preaching, I so often alluded to slavery, and denounced it, that a considerable excitement came to exist among the people." [48]

In England the slave trade was finally abolished in 1807, which followed after the period of Wesley and Whitfield, but also was the year when another revival was born; that of the Primitive Methodists starting with an amazing outpouring of the Spirit at Mow Cop, Cheshire on 31 May.

Wesley himself founded orphanages having first seen them

---

[48]   Lewis A Drummond *Charles Grandison Finney and the Birth of Modern Evangelism* P 202 Hodder and Stoughton

in operation in Germany when he visited Count Zinzendorf and the Moravians. Likewise his contemporary in Wales, Howell Harris supervised similar institutions in the principality.

The prison reformers, Elizabeth Fry and John Howard, were influenced by the revival as was Robert Raikes founder of the Sunday School movement. Social reform at all levels came into being during the times of revival, as the consciences of men and women became alive to the needs all around them. The formation of the trade union movement, the foundation of many educational establishments, industrial reform including abolishing the use of child and female labour in the mines, hospitals and asylums all were influenced at the time of revival otherwise known as the Evangelical Awakening.

Many of the institutions and benefits which we enjoy today owe their existence to those times in previous centuries when God took hold of the church and came upon it like an avalanche with His Spirit.

One of the lasting impacts of the 1859 revival is the Salvation Army. It was in 1861 that William Booth who along with his wife Catherine had been profoundly affected by the revival went to the poverty stricken East End of London. As an evangelist he started to wage war, as he described it, on the devil and all his forces. The original name of his organisation was *The Christian Revival Association*, and it was later changed to the Salvation Army. With his small band of helpers his ministry was in words and deeds, evangelism and social action. His fearless thrust into the evils of society, at great cost to both himself and his workers, changed conditions for the working class in ways never before experienced. The Salvation Army was a result and a continuation of the revival and it has become a byword for Christian action ever since.

It is interesting to read copies of the Salvation Army newspaper *The War Cry* from back in the nineteenth century. In language peculiar to its day it describes graphically some of the early meetings which had all the hallmarks of revival. I have a copy of one such report, concerning Williams Booth's personal envoy, Colonel McKie and his mission in Melbourne, Australia 1891. As the Colonel addressed the meeting, so it appears that the Holy Spirit came down on the gathering with extraordinary results.

"The result of this powerful Holy Ghost talk was that as soon as the opportunity arrived, the tables were crowded with seekers, then the forms at the sides, and again and again they kept coming. Prayer and singing were kept up and intermingled with groans and cries of the seekers. One man, fell at the penitent form, another, a lassie, rushed out with sobs and threw herself at the feet of Jesus. Everybody was jumping, singing, shouting, praying and laughing for the very joy, and when at a quarter to eleven, the Colonel closed, ninety four had knelt seeking salvation, purity and God. Truly it was a marvellous time." [49]

Interest is stirred in World Mission

The modern missionary movement is often traced back to the revival amongst the Moravians in 1727. As God met with this group of Christians in Germany, He stirred them to commence a continuous chain of prayer which was to last for one hundred years. Four years after the commencement of that marathon prayer meeting, which continued twenty-four hours a day, they started to thrust out missionaries into the world scene. By the year 1792 some three hundred missionaries had been sent to all parts of the then known world. This is an even more remarkable fact when one considers the limited means of transport and

49   *The War Cry* 1891

communication available to them. Missionary work then was a lifetime calling!

It was Moravian missionary Peter Boehler who challenged the Wesley brothers on their journey to America. Under God this started a chain of events leading to their conversion and then the evangelisation of England.

Other missionary societies were founded in the eighteenth century including the Baptist Missionary Society and the London Missionary Society, all of which were influenced by the Moravians.

Perhaps the greatest missionary surge forward came in the latter half of the nineteenth century following the 1859 revival. Hudson Taylor was one so influenced and in 1864 the China Inland Mission was founded. Mary Slessor and many other pioneer missionary heroes came from this era.

It was the same from the 1904 revival; this resulted in a stream of missionaries being sent out across the world. Again in the Hebridean revival young men and women were challenged by the great commission and there was another upsurge in missionary candidates.

In Korea today, the thinking of the church is toward world mission and hundreds have been sent from that small Asian country, so touched by revival, to other parts of Asia, Africa, and even South America. The next great missionary surge will not be from western countries but from other lands that have been touched by revival.

One of the reasons for this missionary advance is that God touches the pockets of Christians as well as their hearts, during revival. Mission and social work which previously is not possible due to lack of funds suddenly is able to proceed as Christians rediscover the joy of giving. In times of revival, fortunes are released for the work of God by individual Christians without any outside pressure.

Other Results

The results of revival are legion and only eternity will fully reveal what has been accomplished at these time. There is usually a renewed concern for worship and Christian music which results in the writing of many new hymns and songs. One only has to glance through a hymnbook to see just how many of the hymns we sing today, even in this electronic age, came out of a time of revival.

Charles Wesley, Isaac Watts, Fanny Crosby, to name but a few, are hymn writers whose work has been inspired through times of revival. Their hymns reflect aspects of Biblical truth which are brought back into focus at such times.

Revival brings an increased unity amongst Christians of different persuasions. Revival does not produce new groups, although that often comes in the next generation, but it brings together God's people and differences that have hindered for years become unimportant. This was certainly the case in Wales where churches previously at loggerheads were brought together in services of unity.

Dr. A. Skevington Wood, in a lecture on revival given in 1986, quotes from a French observer of the 1904 revival in Wales:

"It did not create a new sect. It did not raise barriers of hate between people. On the contrary, it reunited them with bonds of charity – Methodists (i.e. Calvinistic Methodists), Baptists

Congregationalists, and Wesleyans have ceased to condemn one another and, in their different chapels, worship the same God.... Evan Roberts preaches a Christianity so wide that it embraces all Christendom."[50]

Dr. Wood goes on to say: "That this is the effect of revival. It brings the true unity of the Spirit. When barriers are re-erected, the blessing is at an end."[51]

Many are called into the Christian Ministry, at such times Bible College and Theological Colleges are overflowing. In November 1904, a young shop worker from Maestag in Wales was converted, his name was George Jeffreys, and he became one of the greatest evangelists of the early twentieth century and founder of the Elim Church. He regularly filled the Royal Albert Hall in London with his meetings.

The reality of revival counteracts the scepticism of modern and liberal theology. There is a renewed interest in Bible reading. Selwyn Hughes quotes one man involved in the Irish revival:

"I used to read the Bible before revival came, but after I came in touch with the Holy Spirit the Bible became a new and different book. It was as if God had taken me up to Heaven, rewritten it and handed it back to me. I know it is inspired because it inspires me."[52]

During the revival in Wales at the beginning of the twentieth century, at one time stocks of all Bibles, both in English and Welsh were sold out.

---

50   J. Rogues de Fursac *Un mouvement Mystique contemporain: le reeil religieux Du Pays de Galles 1904-5* (1907) P183, Quoted by Dr. A. Skevington wood in Lecture on Revival at the Methodist Conference 1986

51   ibid

52   Selwyn Hughes *Every Day With Jesus* May/June 1989

Family life is enriched as those previously consumed with alcohol and other substances become sober. Cartoons appeared in the newspapers around the time of the Welsh revival depicting families reunited. One such cartoon reproduced in *The Christian Herald* on 16 February 1905 depicts a family seated around the table at Christmas with a Father Christmas figure saying "This is a very different scene to that of last year!"

We could go on, the list is almost endless, but that is the wonder of revival.

Revival in any age has brought benefits to both God's people and the community at large. Values and attitudes are completely changed as God accomplishes at a stroke what men have struggled to achieve in seeking to bring some sort of order in a chaotic world. Every generation benefited from revival, it brings God's people back into true relationship with Him and brings a glimpse of Heaven into our very dark world.

CHAPTER 8

Opposition to Revival

It would be very easy to get the impression that revival was the answer to all our problems and that to live in such a time is idyllic bliss. It is true, as our chapter on the results of revival has revealed, that many insurmountable problems are solved and society in general benefits from such a period, but that is only one part of the picture.

In time of revival problems hitherto unforeseen are created, and the work of God is attacked with a force not previously experienced. The early church itself is a classic example, as this newborn church grew under the power of the Holy Spirit so a wave of persecution was unleashed upon it. There may be an immeasurable outpouring of the power of God in revival which will delight the hearts of God's people, but Satan will not sit back and just allow this to happen. As the Prince of Darkness, he loves to have men and women bound in darkness as he exercises his usurped authority on earth, and he hates to see them exposed to the light of God's presence and goodness as this is an undoing of all his evil works. Although a defeated enemy, he will not go down without a fight and will continue to bring the fiercest opposition to the church until the time when he is finally cast into eternal darkness.

During the Second World War, there rose to fame amongst the German ranks one who became almost legendary in his exploits, Field Marshall Erwin Rommel, commander of the Afrika Korps. Although his military career was distinguished in many arenas of the war he is perhaps best remembered for the North African campaign. In 1941, as Allies advanced against the occupying Italian forces, so Rommel was dispatched by the German High Command to this desert region to retake territory and maintain a stronghold for the Axis. His military tactics were brilliant and from early 1941 until June 1942 he swept all before him forcing the British 8th Army eastward until just Alamein remained as an obstacle before him. On the other side, Churchill was determined to see that Alamein was not only held but Rommel defeated in order that the planned invasion of Algeria and Morocco by the Americans in October could take place. Churchill's masterpiece was to appoint Montgomery as commander of the 8th army. Montgomery boosted the flagging moral of the British forces by employing fresh tactics. The battle for Alamein swung rapidly in the favour of the Allies and Rommel himself wrote to his wife early in the campaign to say, "Holding on to our Alamein positions has given us the severest fighting we've seen in Africa."

It was as the Allied forces were posed for victory that Rommel made a counter attack in a last bid attempt at regaining territory. This attack commenced on 31 August 1942 and it was soon apparent to Rommel that victory was not possible due to lack of fuel and supplies. On 23 October, Montgomery unleashed his final attack which not only defeated the German forces but also established a turning point in the war.

Such are the fortunes of war and one could look at many battle scenarios and see a similar pattern develop with constant attack and counter attack. The Christian Church is involved in spiritual warfare and just as the Allied forces were enjoying this period of victory so Rommel launched his counter offensive, so when the church is enjoying a period of revival, Satan launches an all-out attack.

We should never underestimate our enemy. Satan is a master at strategy, he moves swiftly and deceptively to take us unaware when we are experiencing the richest of God's blessing upon our lives. His purpose is always to destroy and undermine the work of God, to distract God's people from their primary task and to discredit the name of God. God can and will look after His own name and He will protect His people but nevertheless they must be aware of his schemes which are heightened in times of revival.

We have previously mentioned the great events of 1858/9 when God poured out His blessing upon America, then the British Isles, and then across the whole world. It could be argued that this was the greatest sweep of revival the world has ever known. Millions were brought to know Christ and the church was revitalised as a spirit of prayer infected the church in epidemic proportions. Most of the world was affected either directly through the church or through missionary endeavours. It was however when Christianity was enjoying such prominence that Satan subtly moved to draw the attention away from the great work of God.

1859 will always be remembered by Christians as the year of the great revival. Dr. Martyn Lloyd –Jones preached a series of sermons on *Revival* in 1959 to celebrate what he called "the unusual outpouring and manifestation of the Spirit of God ", that took place one hundred years previous in 1859. However another event occurred in that year which was to shake the world and have ripple effects through subsequent generations. The English naturalist Charles Robert Darwin (1809-82) published his famous work, *The Origin of the Species by means of Natural Selection.* He propounded the theory of evolution, which was that organisms tend to produce offspring varying from one generation to another, and "natural selection" favours those best adapted to their environment. These factors he concluded produce in subsequent generations a species very different to its ancestor and from this process all life form has evolved.

This revolutionary work rocked the church as it was seen as a direct attack upon God as Creator and the Biblical record in Genesis. Whilst the theory has been debated ever since without definite conclusion, it sowed seeds of doubt in countless minds as to the nature of man and more important that of God. Darwin, probably unwittingly, opened the door to an all-out attack upon God and the Bible which had never previously been questioned. Darwin's theories may today still cause much debate and even conflict but his publication unleashed a wave of liberal teaching that has so weakened the church. The essence of his theory on the evolution of species is today considered normal teaching in the educational system in the western world.

Such was the master plan of Satan to cause havoc in the thinking of the church and have the world remember not a great revival but a scientist's theory.

Again in 1861 the impact of the revival was to be threatened from another quarter. This time not so much in a direct attack on the church but by an event that was to focus the world's attention for the next four years and ultimately divert the course of history; the American Civil War. Nowhere was there greater blessing than in America during 1858, with around one million added to the church and another million revitalised, and maybe this was preparation for the terrible events about to take place as the nation went to war. The impact of the 1858 revival on America can never be lost, but again attention is drawn from this great event and history focuses on the bloody years of 1861-65. Prayer meetings did continue through the Civil war, often on the battlefield itself, but the terrible toll of the war wrenched the heart from the nation and the impetus of 1858 passed away.

Satan cannot let revival pass by without some counter attack, he could never undo the great works of 1858/9 for they were of God, but he did his very best to spoil them.

The story is similar in Korea. In 1907 revival took place in Pyongyang which changed the nature of the church in that country and also laid the foundation for all that God was to do in subsequent years. Within two years of the revival, the Japanese Armies invaded the country inflicting heavy casualties on the population and severe persecution upon the church. Incredibly as church history shows so often, the church thrived on this persecution but again we see how revival attracts the attention of Satan.

In the revival since the Korean War (1950-53), although persecution has never been far away, Satan has used other tactics. He has produced a counterfeit religion which has attracted far more attention in the media than the true church of God in Korea. The new messiah was the Rev. Sun Moon, founder of the Moonies or the Unification Church, which has enslaved millions of adherents the world over, especially among young people. His antics and his empire have attracted much attention particularly from the sensational side of the media and caused a backlash on religion, especially Christianity.

Satan will not let the good work of God go unhindered, his tactics in Korea may be changing in even more sinister ways, but we can only expect this when he sees the church as God intends it to be, which reminds him of his defeat by Christ.

Every period of revival encounters opposition of one sort or another and any honest record of revival will make mention of it. In fact it is probably true to say that one would have to question the true nature of a revival if there was no opposition. It is only to be expected and should be taken into careful consideration when praying for revival; if we do not we are being unrealistic and could be disappointed when it happens. The most surprising element to the opposition encountered in revival is that in most cases, the strongest and most vitriolic attacks come from the church itself and often that from godly men and women.

In the days of Wesley and Whitfield, it was the established church that attacked them and eventually put them outside its bounds. It was never Wesley's intention to create a rival denomination to the Anglican Church; in fact he remained all his life a loyal supporter of it. The Methodist Movement grew up through the ever increasing group of converts, who were themselves denied access to the established church.

The church leaders poured scorn on Wesley and his methods as they only revealed the superficiality and ineffectiveness of their own. The Evangelical Revival initially centred around Bristol where hundreds of the working classes came to faith in Christ. The Bishop of Bristol at that time was Joseph Butler (1692-1752), a godly man himself who deplored the state of the nation and the secularisation of the church. He preached reform and return to true faith, yet he was violently opposed to the Wesley brothers. Bishop Butler unlike so many of his contemporaries adhered to the historic faith, was a believer in the correct sense of the word and from a logical standpoint could have been Wesley's ally, but it was he who banned him from preaching in the pulpits of his diocese. In retrospect, it is hard to understand, but it is all too frequently the case in revival let alone at other times that the church cares more for its divisions than its commission.

A similar case is that of Jonathan Edwards, the preacher God used to bring about a mighty revival across New England in the early 18th Century. During the revival which started in 1734, 50,000 were added to the church out of a total population of 250,000. His sermons and writings were distributed to great effect both far and near and are still considered by many today to be classics on revival. One of the reasons for Edwards taking up his pen was to answer the growing tide of criticism against the revival. It seems incredible in those days when the presence of God was so real amongst His people, that this should be the case.

The criticism gradually weakened the work, so that eventually Edwards turned his pen from his critics to the very problems now being created within revival itself.

The saddest episode of all in his life must have been when he was put out of his church, where there had been so much blessing, by his own church members on 22 June 1750. Such is the course of revival with no guarantee of security for those whom God chooses to use.

The great Scottish preacher William Burns and friend of Robert Murray M'Cheyne, who saw mighty outpourings of God's Spirit through his ministry in Kilsyth and Inverness during the 1840s, was subjected to a gruelling examination of his work from his fellow ministers.

Charles Finney, who constantly moved in revival during the 19th Century, was attacked by both Christians and non-Christians alike. In 1826, as revival swept through Oneida, effigies of Finney and his colleagues were hung in public and at meetings opposition crowds gathered in an endeavour to drown with noise the preacher's message. Stones were frequently thrown at the buildings where meetings took place and at times even gunshots were fired. The more subtle and dangerous opposition came again from the church and in particular a Rev. William Weeks who undermined the work of the revival in a series of published pamphlets. Parties hitherto divided in the church came together in a united attack on Finney's methods and they seemed to have no scruples in distorting the truth. Attacks continued throughout his lifetime but they are all overshadowed by the results accomplished by God through his ministry.

During the Welsh Revival of 1904, Evan Roberts was scurrilously attacked in the press by a fellow clergyman, Rev. Peter Price. He was accused of hallucinations and mysticism, to which accusations he never responded publicly, but those who knew him best said that he was profoundly affected by this criticism. After the peak of the revival in 1905, Roberts withdrew from the public eye and in 1907 suffered severe nervous exhaustion. Never again was this man, so greatly used of God, to take a place in public ministry. It could well be argued that this unfounded criticism brought this revival to an early end and severely crippled one of its leaders under God.

In 1949, there was the revival in the Hebrides commonly known as the "Lewis Awakening". Duncan Campbell of the Faith Mission was God's instrument on this occasion, under his preaching many came under the power of God and repentance became the order of the day in that community. Campbell was however attacked by Rev. Kenneth Macrae, a free Presbyterian minister, for his theological leanings to the Arminian stance. It is quite remarkable that Macrae should take this line as he himself had been used in a large awakening during his ministry in Scotland. He denied that in Lewis and its surrounding area there was any evidence of the revival, and he accused Campbell of exaggeration.

When God is at work there is always an abundance of critics and godly and ungodly men alike are only too happy to rationalise revival and its effects.

The words of the old prophet Simeon come to mind in this context, when giving his blessing to the infant Jesus he says:

"This child is destined to cause the falling and rising of many in Israel, and to be a sign that will be spoken against, so the thoughts of many hearts will be revealed. And a sword will pierce your own soul too." (Luke 2:34-5)

Mary would understand the meaning of this prophecy in

later years when this same Jesus was crucified but how true also is it that wherever Jesus is uplifted and His church is brought to the fore; it becomes a "sign that is spoken against".

The psychiatrist, John White who has carefully studied the subject of revivals has noted that when they occur there is always opposition. He says:

"The irony of revivals is that while they are so longed for in times of bareness, they are commonly opposed and feared when they arrive." [53]

He also says:
"Opposition to revival comes not just from sinners but from Christian leaders, some of them godly and respected leaders. And in this sense, revival causes division. The hostility in never to the idea of revival, which is ardently prayed for, but to God's answer to our prayers and the unexpected form it may take." [54]

Why then, if revival brings such blessing and increase to the church and the community at large, do men and women oppose it? As I have looked at the history of revival, I have discovered four reasons which can account for it. There are in all probability several others as well.

Jealousy

There are many people who earnestly pray for revival, but somehow they want it on their terms. Maybe they want it to be in their church or in a certain locality, or in some particular way. The fact is that revival only comes on God's terms, He is sovereign and it comes to the place of His choosing and His own

53   John White *When the Spirit comes with power.* P39 Hodder and Stoughton
54   ibid

peculiar way. Sometimes God misses the established church and the place we consider more important so that He can work in His way.

I quoted previously, Dr.Judson Cornwall on a visit to the United Kingdom saying; "If you pray for revival, don't be surprised if it comes to the church down the road, that is a true test of Christian character!"

Countless hundreds have prayed for an outbreak in Europe during the twentieth century and God answered those prayers but not in the way that most would have expected. It was not to England, Scotland, Wales or Ireland this time, or even across the English Channel in France, Germany, Belgium, Austria, Switzerland or any other European nations. God chose to come to a people within the borders of all those countries, a people with strong ties and identity yet were not hemmed in by human-made borders. Revival came in the 1950s to the Romany people and it spread amongst them through every nation of Europe and beyond. They had a common language with no barriers to hold them and it swept on the like a prairies fire. It started in Brittany in 1952 and the growth of the church among these people was described as "like that of New Testament days". With such a mobile population it is difficult to be accurate with numbers, but independent observers estimated there to be around 40,000 baptised members by 1977. A revival of this nature may never hit the headlines, but that so often is God's way of working.

Tom Wilson, himself a gypsy, in his book *The Secret Revival* says:

"It is the greatest revival, because simultaneously in every country in the world God has moved by His Spirit and sovereignly saved a people unto Himself. This wonderful move of God started in France and has spread all over the world at present to 45 countries. Yes you hear of revivals in one country at a time, but where have you heard of one worldwide?" [55]

When revival comes many of God's people do not like the place or the manner of it, and because it has not happened how they wanted it, they are fired with jealousy.

Robert Murray M'Cheyne is a wonderful example of how to handle revival in such circumstances. In 1836, when he began his ministry in Dundee, he prayed earnestly for revival and whilst he saw many results he did not see revival. In 1839, due to ill-health, he was sent by his doctor to Israel to recover and he left the church in the capable hands of fellow minister and friend William C. Burns. It was whilst he was away in Israel under the ministry of Burns that revival broke out in the church and spread through Scotland. M'Cheyne heard the news in Israel and it was reported that his heart rejoiced. Andrew Bonar his biographer said of him:

"He had no envy at another instrument having been so honoured in the place where he himself had laboured with many tears and temptations. In true Christian magnanimity, he rejoiced that the work of the Lord was done, by whatever hand." [56]

As we may pray again for revival in our day, and rightly we might want it in our church or situation, we must face the fact that God in His wisdom may send it elsewhere. How then might we react?

---

55   Tom Wilson *The Secret Revival* P1 Published 1999
56   Luis Palau *Scottish Fires of Revival* P65 D.I.M.E.

Busyness

Another danger is that our being too busy, even about God's work that we miss out when He moves. Church life is so often a round of activities, committee meetings, with schedules and goals to be kept, none of which in themselves are wrong until they become the sum total of church life. It is all too easy to become taken up with what we are doing so that it becomes all-important to us.

In some situations where God has wonderfully worked, ministers have been asked to scrap all the many meetings and activities in the church and just spend time in prayer before God. Sadly, the prayer meeting is often the first meeting to go in the church because we are so busy with other activities.

I remember speaking with an African evangelist who had personally experienced revival in more than one African nation and he said this; "When God moves, our well planned programmes are scrapped." The question we need to ask is whether our programmes are so important that they will blind us from seeing a true move of God.

Dislike

We have previously mentioned that unusual occurrences may take place during revival. They may not always be to our liking or in some ways suit our tradition, they can upset the system. Many times during revival both men and women have been thrown prostrate on the floor. This is not the sort of behaviour one would expect in respectable church circles and it may even be a little frightening, but it is God that is now at work, not us. Miracles and healing take place that can go against our theological preference, but it is God at work.

In the 1859 revival in Ulster, it is recorded that children were greatly used during the revival. Prayer meetings would take place in the playgrounds and children themselves became evangelists even to their teachers. Such things might well be frowned upon in our modern, protective society.

Many who have prayed for revival have not liked it when it has come, which has resulted in opposition. Jonathan Edwards is quoted as saying:

"People are very ready to be suspicious of what they have not felt themselves. It is to be feared many good men have been guilty of this error. These persons that thus make their own experience their rule of Judgement, instead of bowing to the wisdom of God are guilty of casting a great reflection upon the understanding of the most High."[57]

If we try to put God in our box and expect Him to work as He has in the past or in the way we want Him to, then we also may not like it when revival comes!

Rejection

One further danger is the outright rejection of revival when it comes. Let me explain. There are some people who pray for revival but they do not really want it. Their reasons for praying may be many and varied, it may just seem the right thing to do or it may even be doing something for them in bolstering their own self-esteem. Whatever the reason, the fact is when it comes they do not want to change and change we surely must, with revival!

We have to be honest enough to face this danger, if we want our home life, our church life, our work life, our social life to stay the same; we should not pray for revival! None of God's people

---

57   Jonathan Edwards quoted by Martyn Lloyd-Jones in *The Puritan Experiment*

can remain unchanged when they have experienced revival and such changes may be painful. If change is not on our agenda, with regard to prayer, holiness of living and deep concern for the lost, then neither can be revival. A careful examination of our motives is needed; otherwise we may be guilty of rejecting God's powerful and wonderful work when it comes.

Revival will certainly bring opposition of one sort or another; of this we may be sure. As we however pray for it to come we must heed the dangers, less we become that very opposition.

CHAPTER 9

Preparation for Revival

When a city or country is under attack from an enemy and defeat appears to be imminent, it can take one of two courses of action; it can either sit back and allow the inevitable to happen, hoping all the while that some rescue attempt will be made from outside, or it can make preparations from within so as to make a rescue attempt from outside easier and more within the bounds of possibility.

When a nation is crumbling from moral and spiritual decay, and disaster seems to be around the corner, the church can either sit back and hope that at the last moment God will intervene, or it can make preparations with the full expectation that revival will come.

If revival is a real possibility, what preparations can we as a church be making in anticipation? In one sense there is nothing we can do considering that revival is a sovereign act of God. However, alongside the sovereignty of God always goes the responsibility on the part of God's people. This is not to say that we can engineer a revival; or make it an absolute certainty, but there are certain actions that can be taken which have in the past been the forerunners to revival. God is the only guarantee for revival, whatever we do will never guarantee it, we can only hope and pray that God takes notice of our earnestness and has mercy on us once again.

Dr. Walter Kaiser in his book, *Quest for Revival* makes this comment on the debate regarding the sovereignty of God and the responsibility of man in revival:

"I conclude that there can be no revival without the Lord's initiating it and carrying it out. But I also concluded that no one can hide behind the doctrine of God as the explanation for why we have not had revival in our day or the reason that the last great revival in America occurred in 1905/6. There are requisite factors for revival, such as prayer, the preaching of the Word of God, humbling ourselves under the mighty hand of God, and earnestly seeking His face."[58]

Dr. Stephen Olford, who preached on revival over many years likens the church to a sailing ship becalmed upon the sea There is absolutely nothing the crew can do to make the ship move for it is entirely dependent upon the wind. They can however, set the sails so that when the wind blows again, the ship will be ready to take full advantage of the wind and thus be able to complete its voyage. We may not be able to change the situation ourselves, indeed we are dependent upon outside help, but we can set the sails so when the wind of the Holy Spirit blows the church will be ready to move under His direction.

1 Peter 2:11-12 speaks about "the day God visits us", implying an inevitability that He will visit the church in revival. The emphasis in the passage of Scripture is however about the way in which God's people should be living in preparation for that day. Peter urges his readers that in spite of all the pressures from the world around they should seek to live holy lives so when God comes upon them in all His power, those who have scorned and even persecuted will turn to Him.

There is therefore preparation in practical ways we can make as we look forward to visitation from God in revival. Here are some suggestions as to ways in which God's people, both as individuals and as a church can make such preparation.

---

58   Walter Kaiser *Quest for Renewal* P24-5 Moody Press

Recognise the need for revival.

There is a great temptation as we see both the state of the world and the church to say, "What can I do about the situation?" Many are led into a state of sheer frustration by the hopelessness all around. It is understandable that some Christians just become resigned to things how they are and feel that nothing can be done to bring about change.

It is however that very hopelessness which God can use to stir within us a desire for revival. What needs to happen is we recognise that revival is the only answer, the only real hope to turn the situation around. This is surely the message of 2 Chronicles 7:13-14; when the situation becomes really desperate, God's people have no alternative but to come before Him in humility and pray for His mercy again in revival.

Dr. Martyn Lloyd-Jones used this phrase, "We need to come to a point of godly desperation." It is this sense of desperation that Jesus echoes over the seven churches in Revelation 2 & 3; in particular the church at Laodicea. In this letter there is that sense of pleading with the church to return to Him, in order that it might know the blessing of true fellowship. In the same way individuals, as they recognise how desperate the church has once again become before her Master, need to plead with God on her behalf.

The longing for revival needs to become the preoccupation of individuals in the church. It needs to be preached from the pulpits and prayed for in the quiet places for the sake of the church and the world at large.

The Principality of Wales experienced a great revival in 1859, yet prior to that in the year 1858 the church was described as in a state of deadness. Immorality and other sinful practices had been imbibed from the world so that they were openly carried out in the church. The church had become oblivious to the needs around and failed to preach its message of hope to a generation heading for a lost eternity. There was no sense of "burden" in the poorly attended prayer meetings and preaching had become empty and entertaining. One man stands out at that time, his name was David Morgan, there were others but he particularly was used by God at that time. It was said of this man that for ten years before 1858 a petition for the outpouring of the Holy Spirit was never absent from his public prayers.

An entry in his diary in 1855 reads as follows:

"It is a big thing to have a feeling that God would revive His work. Whoever possesses such a feeling will be compelled to do all he can to revive the Lord's work. By reading the history of the church we find that the great cause fluctuates up and down through the ages, but that, whenever the Lord drew near to save there was some considerable expectancy amongst the godly for his coming. As well as praying, we should be doing our utmost to revive the work. So did the godly of old, they prayed and they worked." [59]

May God grant His people today, such a passion for revival that they will not give up until an outpouring such as swept Wales in 1859 takes place.

Leonard Ravenhill, a British evangelist born in 1907, was trained for the ministry at Cliff College in England. He was a powerful preacher and stirred slumbering congregations both in his native country and America to call on God for revival. His book *"Why Revival Tarries"*, is a classic challenge to the Christian to wake up before it is too late. In one of his messages he says:

"Whether we want another Pentecost or not, we need it. We need God to send another cauldron of heavenly lava, spilling out from another upper room to another moribund church group."[60]

Keep Christ central in our activities

As we pray for revival, Christ must always be kept at the centre of our lives. If revival restores the church to relationship with the Living Christ as it should be, then in preparation we should ensure that He is firmly in focus. We can get caught up so easily with all manner of activities, both in and out of the church that the One who should be at the centre is unconsciously moved to one side. Personalities can become all important and almost without realising we give to them more prominence than Christ. Even our desire for revival itself can become the focal point of our attention and we may forget that Jesus Christ and honouring His name is the purpose of revival.

During the East African revival, which broke out in 1935, one man who God used amongst others was an African evangelist named William Ngenda. When he came to England he found Christians looking at revival almost as some mystical experience. He was horrified at this and said:

"For me it's Jesus, right in the centre! All that stems from Him – light, fellowship, revival, healing, tongues, even salvation itself radiates out of Him. If once you take any one of those and put that in the centre, Jesus gets out of focus and you begin to get error." [61]

How right he was, for revival is not about the phenomena that may occur, or the great crowds, or wonderful stories of conversion, or the unity of believers or anything else that God

60   Leonard Ravenhill *Sodom had no Bible* P64   Fires of Revival
61   Bill Butler *Hill Ablaze* P80 Hodder and Stoughton

might do; it is putting Jesus back in the centre of our thinking, our praying, our preaching and our very lives. We can therefore start the process by seeing that it happens now and not allowing other things however legitimate they might be to crowd Him out.

As we anticipate revival with Jesus at the centre, so also there needs to be a re-emphasis upon the Cross of the Lord Jesus. When revival comes it will be the Cross that men and women will fall before with tears of both repentance and joy. At times, when the church has been on the downward spiral, it has also been a time when the preaching of the Cross has not been emphasised and sadly the message has often been watered down.

Far too many preachers are able to impress their congregations with superb oratory and intellectual ability. The ears of the hearers are tickled with fine words which may bring pleasure and comfort but never repentance and tears. If revival is to come preachers must stop short-changing their congregations and start to preach the Cross again. It is not popular and it may be a matter of losing status, but the Cross was never meant to be popular.

In 1903, it is interesting to note from the records available to us, that in this period leading up to the Welsh Revival all over the nation preachers began to preach again the message of the Cross. At meetings and conferences the call went out for "direct preaching of the Cross". At the Keswick Convention that same year the speakers with a Divine uniformity spoke on the Cross. It was a memorable convention as the Holy Spirit swept over that vast gathering with life changing results. A report in the *"Life of Faith"* captured the spirit of those meetings:

"The writer heard Christians of long-standing declare they had never before realised how awful and humiliating was the death of Christ. Two great truths were set forth among us – first, that Christ died for us; second that we are identified with Him in death. To thousands of Christians the second point was an aspect of the work of Christ that hitherto had escaped their notice. Here was the secret of rest and power in a word."[62]

It is also interesting to note that back in 1902 prophetic words were given concerning the coming revival, but that it would not come until "the word of the Cross" was preached again.

In preparation for revival the Cross of Jesus must be preached again for both non-Christian and Christian alike; for the one to show him where his need can be met, and the other to remind him of where he stands and the cost involved. This was the Apostle Paul's message in 1 Corinthians 2:2, and it must be that of the church to prepare for revival.

The possibility of revival will become more and more reality as we emphasise the centrality of Christ and His Cross.

Pray for revival

What more can be said about prayer? In one sense prayer is all we can do in preparation for revival and without it, whether from a few intercessors or the church as a whole, there will be no revival. We may look on enviously at the growing church in Korea and other nations, including China, but let us not forget that these are praying churches. Prayer mountains abound over Korea, and when you see people eagerly waiting to attend prayer meetings you realise this is a dimension that is missing from the church in the western world. Statistics are not always accurate from China but it has been estimated that every morning at 5 a.m., up to one million Chinese Christians are at prayer.

---

62   *Life of Faith* 1905 Quoted by Jessie Penn-Lewis in *Awakening in Wales* P20
         Overcomer Trust

Every revival has its foundation in prayer, and prayer has been the central activity of them, sometimes as in 1858 when it was almost the only feature.

Cotton Mather (1663-1727) is considered to be the "father" of the Awakening at the beginning of the eighteenth century in New England. He was from an influential family, a scholar, diplomat, and pastor who was widely recognised throughout the colony. His great burden was for revival and he devoted 490 days and nights to prayer for revival in New England. He died in 1727 never seeing the revival for himself. But in 1727 Jonathan Edwards started his ministry and under his powerful preaching the wind of the Spirit began to blow across the colony. Richard Lovelace, an American theologian and historian, says that where there is prayer, revival cannot be far behind.

Prayer for revival is costly and time consuming, but unless there are men and women like Cotton Mather who are committed to intercessory prayer raised up, it is doubtful whether we will ever see revival! We may have the best organisation in the world, the finest preachers in our pulpits, we may give fortunes to the work of God, but without prayer it is of little avail. The prayer that brings heaven down to earth will totally consume a man or woman in their intimacy with God. This kind of prayer is not just the weekly prayer meetings or the individual's devotional life; it means the total priority of prayer over everything else. This commitment to prayer has sometimes been considered the lot of those who give themselves to a monastic life, or more often in our evangelical circles that of elderly members who are no longer as active as once they were. That is a fallacy coming from Satan himself, prayer is activity of the highest and most demanding order and has to be at every level of the church's life.

It is only the intercessor who will have such a depth of relationship with God so that he or she can know the mind of

God for revival. It was Peggy Smith, who was eighty four years old and blind, one of the intercessors on the Isle of Lewis who said to Duncan Campbell; "If you were living as near to God as you ought to be, He would reveal His secrets to you also."

It is understood that back in 1944, while Korea was still under Japanese occupation there were women engaged in intercessory prayer for the nation. The massive church growth did not start for another twenty years.

Reality in prayer and revival are partners together, prayer with perseverance and faith therefore must come back as priority in the church and our individual lives before revival comes, and intercessors as in times past must take their place on their knees before God. The words of A. W. Tozer strike with alarming force; "To desire revival and at the same time neglect personal prayer and devotion is to wish one way and walk another."

Men and women like John Knox who cried, "Give me Scotland, or I die!" are needed today.

Be Ready for Change

It was said of Charles Finney that three things stood out in his life; his willingness to change, his deep devotional life and prayer,and his message of practical and immediate holiness.

When God visits His people again in revival we must be a people who are prepared to change. It is often our inflexibility that becomes a barrier to God working in our lives and when we see some of the opposition to revivals in the past it is frightening to realise that this has come about sometimes because men of God have not been prepared to change. When God moves in revival, all of our well-organised programmes are swept aside because God Himself takes over.

This may well upset out timescale, disturb our preachers and cause havoc in our hitherto organised meetings. Many a church would be disturbed if men and women start to cry out in the service and even prostrate themselves on the floor before the holiness of God. When Jonathan Edwards preached his famous sermon, "Sinners in the hands of an angry God", on July 8th 1741, so great was the sense of conviction of sin that strong men cried out to God for forgiveness. In some churches today this would cause such uproar that special leaders' meetings would have to be called.

At Asbury College, Wilmore, Kentucky, in 1970, there was such an outpouring of God's Spirit that a chapel service started at the beginning of a week was still continuing at the end of the week. All lectures were abandoned for that time and unprecedented newsreel footage of the happening was broadcast on television. I am also aware of a similar happening at other Bible Colleges, such outpourings did in minutes what hours of lectures on theology and homiletics could never do.

During Whitfield's meetings, and at the camp meetings at the end of the eighteenth century in America, the scene was sometimes described as looking more like a battlefield than a religious meeting. The Primitive Methodist movement came to birth around 1801 and as hundreds gathered on a hill called Mow Cop in Cheshire, the singing, praying , preaching was totally unconventional and as such the like had never been seen before in the land.

No two revivals have been the same and we certainly cannot dictate or even imagine as to how God will work again, we must therefore be flexible and be ready if necessary to throw overboard practices and positions that may have become dear to us. Much of church life today is governed by committees and meetings, in revival it is a people totally captivated by God! As on the day of Pentecost, there is an element of surprise in the working of the Holy Spirit, so God may surprise us again and it may mean changing our traditions, our preconceived ideas of God and even revival itself!

Be prepared for the cost

There is one issue that must be faced squarely as we seek God for revival, which is the cost involved. Revival along with all its many blessings, is above all, costly for God's people. They are likely to be misunderstood, considered fanatical and even persecuted. To pray for revival is very serious business and should not be undertaken lightly, the possible consequences must be considered very carefully.

In order to procure our salvation, it cost Jesus everything, for it meant the Cross! To go through with God for revival may cost us everything, the words of Jesus in Matthew 16:24-26 take on new meaning as we pray and work for it.

It will certainly cost our pride and status; it may cost our work, health, time, money, and possibly for some even their life. Tears by the gallon will have to flow for this lost world and the indifferent church.

Those whom God has used as instruments in revival have suffered greatly for their stance and actions.

John Wesley lost the pulpits of the Established Church. Jonathan Edwards was put out of the church that he had served so faithfully. David Brainerd's health failed and he died at the age of twenty-nine. Hugh Bourne and Williams Clowes, in England, at the beginning of the nineteenth century were attacked by mobs. Robert Murray M'Cheyne of Dundee died like Brainerd at the age of twenty-nine.

Revival will always exact its toll, it is not the road for those who want to be superstars, it is the way for those who are prepared to suffer for the sake of Christ.

An incident in the life of Evan Roberts of Wales illustrates something of the cost. An eye witness records that Roberts, a man of deep prayer, asked God to give him a "taste of Gethsemane" and he describes how in the pulpit Roberts was totally overcome with grief, falling to the floor as one mortally wounded, he shook physically under such anguish. It was a frightening experience for all who observed and afterwards it was evident to them that he had passed through something that was extremely costly.

In an earlier chapter it was mentioned how within two years of the Welsh Revival, Roberts suffered a form of breakdown and never again during his life would he have a public ministry.

Duncan Campbell's biographer tells of how this man of God at the peak of the Hebridean Revival was overcome by inexplicable darkness for a period of three months. It was a humbling experience for Campbell and he concluded it was so that God could teach him to seek no personal glory from the work he had been given to do.

There is a price to pay for revival as it is very serious business.

There are three other practical suggestions to help in preparation for revival. The first is to read widely on the subject from accounts of the past and probably more important of what God is doing around the world today. In parts of the world, the church is experiencing revival and it is sometimes difficult to keep up with pace of developments.

Secondly, as we catch the vision for revival it is beholden upon us to stir up others with this same vision. Few in the church have genuine interest and vision for revival; they need encouragement from those who do have it.

Thirdly, we need to be patient, we do not know when God will move, and we have to face the fact that like others we may not see it in our lifetime. Cotton Mather died before the Great Awakening. Others have prayed and not seen it happen but those prayers have been deposited in the bank of Heaven.

God's timing is never the same as ours, we however need to be ready for the moment when He moves from Heaven and in the meantime continue in all of our evangelistic efforts as we have been commissioned.

Before leaving our thoughts about preparation for revival, there is one other matter to consider: the grace of God! We do not deserve revival. It is not our right, it is God's privilege. We like the prophet Habakkuk of old can in the end only appeal to God for His mercy.

> "Lord, I have heard of your fame, I stand in awe of your deeds, O Lord. Renew them in our day, in our time make them known; in wrath remember mercy." (Habakkuk 3:2)

There is no way in which we can justify a case to God for revival, for in every generation we are the same, a people who in spite of what God has done in the past, turn our back on Him, time and time again. When God sends revival it is not because of His people, it is out of His mercy and in order to honour His name among the nations.

Let us come back to the message God gave to the prophet Ezekiel:

> "Therefore say to the house of Israel, ' This is what the Sovereign Lord says: It is not for your sake, O house of Israel, that I am going to do these things, but for the sake of my holy name, which you have profaned among the

nations where you have gone. I will show the holiness of my great name, which has been profaned among the nations, the name you have profaned among them. Then the nations will know that I am the Lord, declares the Sovereign Lord, when I show myself holy through you before their eyes." (Ezekiel 36:22-23)

When God's people come before Him and genuinely cry out for mercy, then maybe from His boundless store of grace, He will act! From His mercy and grace He has granted revival in the past that will be the source of any fresh revival.

CHAPTER 10

A Plea for Revival

Having looked at the definition of revival, considered its biblical and historical roots, the question we ask now is; "Where does this leave us today?"

Is revival a dream unlikely to be fulfilled in the twenty-first century? Is it unrealistic as it so long since such an event took place in the Western world? Are we deceiving ourselves by looking to the past and how accurate are the accounts? Has the church moved on and such occurrences now considered old fashioned?

It is right we do ask questions and we must be absolutely honest but there is one issue that cannot be ignored. Has God changed, is He still the same God who poured out blessing in Biblical times, is He the same God who has touched the church with revival as recorded in history? If we believe our God is unchanging, as is claimed of Jesus in Hebrews 13:8, then surely He can move again in our generation.

Allow me to indulge in some personal reflection to explain why I am convinced that a vision for revival is not a pipedream but something I had the privilege of witnessing a few years ago.

As far back as I can remember, I have had an interest in revival prompted by stories coming directly out of the revival in the Hebrides around 1949/50. I even heard Duncan Campbell preach, although I can only recall his strong Scottish accent rather than his content. I have read about it, prayed for it, shared about it at various churches and to Bible College students but never experienced it. This was however to change when along with a colleague from the Bible College where I worked we received an invitation to Korea to speak at a number of churches and colleges.

Korea is a fascinating country; having been divided from its neighbour in the north by a bitter war it has established itself as an industrial power through hard work and expertise in technology. Industrial success is but one part of the Korean story; coming from a background of eastern religions it has seen church growth at a rate without parallel in any other part of the world through the twentieth century.

Driving through the suburbs of cities like Seoul or Pusan at night one is immediately struck by the numerous illuminated red crosses standing out across the skyline. This forest of red crosses represents a church that is not only visible but having an impact on society.

I met several pastors and Christian leaders while in Korea and spoke at a variety of churches and theological colleges. Here I found a deeply devoted people committed to prayer and focused on the Lord Jesus.

Along with my colleague, we attended a prayer meeting held on a Friday evening in a theatre. There were several hundred in the packed auditorium, mostly young people. This prayer meeting went on through the night until the early hours of the following morning. It was our understanding that this happened every week and similar gatherings were taking place all over the country.

The event that made the most impact upon me was being invited to an early morning prayer meeting somewhere in Seoul. Our hosts awakening us at just after four in the morning and then drove us at breakneck speed through the streets of the city. As we neared our destination we became aware that we were not the only ones going in this direction. Cars and buses along with numerous pedestrians were all heading towards the church, and still it was before five in the morning. It reminded me of the crowds going to attend football matches on a Saturday afternoon back home, but this was for a prayer meeting. My mind flitted to stories I had read of the Welsh revival in 1904/5 when early in the morning the sound of feet on the cobble stones could be heard as the coal miners walked through the valleys to pray in the chapels before their day's work. Here it was happening again, I was witnessing it, this time in Korea!

Inside the church people were praying everywhere, in the corridors, in the side rooms, even some on top of cupboards, all leading into the overflowing main auditorium. The sight and sound of that vast congregation in prayer is something that will remain with me all my life. I could not understand their language but I knew Heaven was responding to such music. It was a sense of the presence of God as never before experienced; this was Heaven touching Earth. It was a moment to savour in the presence of a Holy God and I could identify with the prophet Isaiah and say; "Woe to me! ... for I am a man of uncleans lips and I live among a people of unclean lips."

We later learned that some six thousand were praying in that church every morning. It was no wonder that the church was growing at a rate of five hundred new converts each month. The pastor, a humble man who had been with the church from its beginning, spoke to us afterwards and said, "It's just God's doing". This was revival and it convinced me that revival is not just something in the history books but can happen today.

The Church Needs Revival

With a few exceptions, the church today in the western world is generally in decline. Church attendance is at an all-time low, prayer meetings have become rare and the Word of God is heard less and less. The values of the world have been imbibed by the church, there is compromise on a whole range of issues both morally and theologically and evangelism has become almost a dirty word.

In many a church there is little difference between the entertainment provided by the media and our Sunday services. Technology has taken over at the expense of godly preparation and prayer. Where is the sense of reverence before an awesome and holy God? Rarely, I believe, in the repetitive singing of self-centred songs!

Of course, we must be relevant to our culture and interest people who have never been in a church building, but if God is not central in our worship then it is to no avail.

If an alien from another planet (if such a being existed!) visited the church, one wonders what impression he would gain. As he went from church to church not only would he be hit by apathy from individuals going through a routine of church, but he would also be met by much division. He would find new groups springing up out of division, others not speaking with each other and even anger and bitterness over sometimes petty-minded matters. If that same alien being read the words of Jesus (assuming he reads!)

"A new commandment I give you: love one another. As I have loved you, so you must love one another. By this will all men know that you are my disciples, if you love one another." (John 13:34-35)

He would probably conclude he had come to the wrong planet.

In some groups the essential doctrines of the Gospel have been compromised and social action (important as it is) has been put in its place. The church, again let me emphasise there are exceptions, seems to slumber on towards apparent oblivion.

While the church has problems from inside, outside the attacks grow more ferocious year upon year. Atheistic academics propound their anti-religion dogma with evangelical zeal, the media takes every opportunity to snipe at the church and the level of blasphemy has reached an all-time low. Other religions such as Islam are on the march gaining ground at an alarming rate.

In society, there is an air of complacency and lack of security as values and standards long held, tumble all around. Our laws, so many based on Scriptural foundations, have been overturned and the consequences for the present are frightening and for the future horrific.

Abortion is now just a matter of course for many today, according to *Christian Concern*[63] Some seven million foetuses have been aborted in the last 46 years. There are now dangerous experiments with embryology with horrendous ramifications for our future. Assisted suicide is now openly discussed and could go the way of the Abortion Act. Traditional marriage between a man and a woman is considered only an option as our moral climate continues to decline. Our education system is in chaos as discipline has long been lost to freedom of the individual.

The picture is depressing to say the least; something must

---

63   *Christian Concern* "The high abortion rate continues with young women at risk." Published 29 May 2012

happen for the sake of the church and society at large. Revival in the church must be the answer even if it comes at the expense of persecution! Godly men and women must surely cry out to God for Him to touch us again with a great and glorious revival.

As we draw our thoughts to a conclusion there is one other passage of Scripture to consider, as it sets before us the case we have to plead before the Father Himself in Heaven.

"I the Lord do not change. So you, O descendants of Jacob, are not destroyed. Ever since the time of your forefathers you have turned away from my decrees and have not kept them. Return to me, and I will return to you, says the Lord almighty.

But you ask, how are we to return?

Will a man rob God, yet you rob me. But you ask, How do we rob you?

In tithes and offerings. You are under a curse – the whole nation of you – because you are robbing me. Bring the whole tithe into the storehouse, that there may be food in my house. Test me in this says the Lord Almighty, and see if I will not throw open the floodgates of Heaven and pour out so much blessing that you will not have room enough for it. I will prevent pests from devouring your crops, and the vines in your field will not cast their fruit, says the Lord Almighty. Then all the nations will call you blessed, for yours will be a delightful land, says the Lord Almighty." (Malachi 3:6-12)

These verses are the grounds for our pleading with God for His blessing again in revival. This prophecy is given to Israel whilst still under the domination of the Persian Empire. The

Temple, had been rebuilt in Jerusalem under the direction of Nehemiah (516 BC), sacrifices had been reintroduced (Malachi 1:8) but the priests had apparently become apathetic towards them and corruption had set in. The offerings had become merely a form of ritual, performed out of a sense of duty with very little thought for the God who instituted them. The precise nature and procedure as had been laid down by God was totally ignored so these offerings became devoid of meaning. It seemed to matter little that God was offered the second best, as once again God's people had become the willing victim of dead religion, in spite of their suffering in the past. The priests at this time appear to have more respect for their Persian governor (Malachi 1:9) than for God himself.

As is always the case when the leaders of God's people fail to give the lead, so the people also fall. The people seeing their priests bringing inferior offering, following after them do exactly the same!

When respect for God and true worship is no longer offered, immorality, corruption and other sin comes in like a flood. Divorce had become common, along with intermarriage with foreigners (Malachi 2:10-16), but the worst of all was their arrogance and effrontery to challenge God for His dealing with them. (Malachi 3:13-15).

The prophet brings to these spiritually dead leaders and people challenges that come in the form of questions directly from God. As each of these questions are directed to them, so they respond back with arrogant and insensitive questions addressed to God.

1:2-5 "How have you loved us?"
1:6-2:9 "How have we shown contempt for your name?"
2:10-16 "Why do we profane the Covenant of our fathers by breaking faith with one another?"

2:17-3:6 "How have we wearied God?"
3:7-12 "How do we rob you?"
3:13-15 "What have we said against you/"

It is quite obvious from these quotations that their concept of a holy God had so dimmed it was almost non-existent. In throwing back these questions to God they seem to be saying; "You are not really serious, we're not that bad!" This privileged people had long forgotten with their settlement for comfort and materialism, the God who thundered at Mount Sinai, the One who brought defeat upon the nation because of the greed and deceit of one man Achan (Joshua 7).

Yet in this, the last recorded prophecy of the Old Testament, as the indictments are brought against Israel, God is reminding them that His love and His grace still extends to them if they will heed His word and repent.

This is the background to the passage (Malachi 3:6-12), where God once again shows His grace to His people Israel. That same grace is extended to His people, the Church now, as the last book of the New Testament also reveals. These verses give the basis whereby God's people at any age may come to Him.

The changeless nature of God (3:6-7)

The first response from God to the questioning of the people is to point out that He has not changed. He is the same God who made covenant promises with them centuries earlier but they are the ones who have constantly wavered and turned away from Him. God reminds them of the pattern down through the ages whereby the blessing of God on one generation has been completely forgotten and even disregarded by the next.

Today the situation is the same, God has not changed, Hebrews 13:8 reminds us that Jesus who brought the messages of hope to the dying churches in Revelation is the same today. We have changed with our sophisticated methods and self-reliance, we have changed with our prayer less lives and our disregard for God's Word, and we have changed in that we have laughed at our predecessor's standards and introduced others that have made us indistinguishable from the rest of the world. It is not God who has changed but us!

The Offer of God (3:7-10)

Having first of all stated this basic fact, God goes on to make a most remarkable offer. "Return to me, and I will return to you."

The Lord knowing the minds of His people then asks a question on their behalf before they can utter it themselves. "How are we to return?" The simple answer is captured in the next verses which can be summarised in two words, "by obedience".

If God is to return to them, then they must be obedient in the way they bring their tithes and offerings to God. They had totally disregarded God's laws by not giving to God their best and in so doing they had become guilty of theft against God Himself. When the offerings were brought to the priests for sacrifice it was the leftover of the flock, the weak and sickly of the herd. God had made it very clear to them in the past (Leviticus 1:3 cf) that only the best was good enough for God as this was an indication of the worship of their heart. Equally with their giving, no longer was it the top of the pile as God had instructed but loose change in their purses after their indulgent spending on pleasure and materialism.

The only way that this people could return to God was in repentance that for many would mean restitution and a total reappraisal of their lives and values. As obedience to God once again became the order of the day, so holiness in their daily living would become the norm. This is what God desired for His people in order that true fellowship with Him might be restored and so they might enjoy life lived at its best and highest level.

Following the call to repentance comes a remarkable challenge from God Himself. One might venture to suggest that this is one of the most incredible statements made by God in the whole of the Scriptures. In verse 10, God effectively says: "Put me to the test" , or, "You do this that I ask and see if I keep my word." This is yet another demonstration of the love of God for His people in that He is prepared to allow them to test Him out in such a way. It is Almighty God putting Himself on the line for those He had created and yet had shown indifference to His love, a foreshadow of Calvary itself.

The result of this test, if the conditions are fulfilled is (v.10), so much blessing that you will not be able to contain it. This is what it appears that God longs for His people, sending blessing from Heaven itself upon them in a mighty torrent, like the waters of a flood. That blessing with all it brings is revival!

As God's people again today we are guilty of robbing God, we have maintained a mere semblance of ritual in the best of our evangelical tradition yet for the most part been cold and indifferent towards Him. We have sung all the right songs and come together in times of celebration, yet at the same time avoided times of prayer both privately and corporately. In keeping with the age in which we live, we have accumulated all manner of materialistic trivia, and yet failed to give to God's work and cared for the poor and underprivileged. Along with Frank Sinatra, the church can sing the song, "I've done it my way!" and all around we can see the results of our independence from God. This list could go on. Of course I am aware of generalisations and as ever there is a remnant few who have not fallen. But honest Christians must admit that we certainly are not the people we should be.

Just over four hundred years before Christ, the call went out to God's people to repent, that same call goes out again almost two thousand years after Christ. May we again heed that call, and so experience for ourselves the wonderful blessing that follows.

The promise of God (3:11-12)

In these next verses, God outlines the nature of the blessing. Protection and preservation of their crops and vines, results in proclamation to the nations round about. In other words, God promises to His people that in response to their obedience, He will restore and revitalise them in blessing and through them bless the nations.

There is no way in which we can detail the blessing which will come from revival. We have no way of knowing how he might work again, and it will probably not be the same kind of blessing as for Israel. We may however, be sure that whatever way the revival comes, it will bring with it a sense of real joy. The church will be so changed that its immediate neighbours and those further afield will ask serious questions, and many will be drawn into the Kingdom. The church will no longer be a forgotten corner of modern life, but will thrust out into all parts of society and the world to fulfil the great commission.

In 1905, in Mukta, India, revival broke out; there were reports of repentance, agony over sin, tears, cries for pardon, and for an outpouring of the Holy Spirit. This is how one such report was given and it follows closely to the pattern in Malachi:

"A baptism of fire within came upon them. They seemed to have their eyes opened to see 'the body of sin' in themselves. Then came a strong realisation of Christ's work upon the Cross; then peace, followed by intense joy. It often took a soul hours to pass through all these experiences. The Lord used the Word greatly. The work went on and a spirit of prayer and supplication for a revival in India was poured out like a flood. The spirit of prayer possessed people. 'Waves of prayer go over the meetings like rolling thunder; hundreds pray audibly together." [64]

The revival continued for over a year, blessing hundreds all over India.

Surely in a world where western society slides deeper and deeper into a moral and spiritual abyss, the church cannot just keep reinventing itself. Something needs to happen by way of intervention from beyond its own resources. The church needs again a moving from God such as has happened in time past but relevant to today. In order for this happen it is the responsibility of God's people to plead the cause before the very Throne of Heaven itself.

It was Christmas Evans who was used to bring revival to Wales at the end of the eighteenth century. He cried to God in what many would consider to be an irreverent manner, that God would do something about the state of the church. He was a man on intimate terms with God, and few would dare to be as bold as him when he said; "It's a shameful thing that You allow things to go on like this. Do anything – do something – and do it soon."

As lightening pierces the sky and with one strike sets a forest ablaze, may God so come down to His church again and set alight such a fire that encompasses the whole earth.
May the ancient prayer be echoed in our day :
"Please Lord, do it again!"

Some helpful books on "Revival"

Bennett, *Howell Harris and the Dawn of Revival*. Evangelical Press of Wales, 1962

Blair and Hunt, *The Korean Pentecost*, Banner of Truth, 1977

Bonar, *Robert Murray M'Cheyne*, Banner of Truth, 1960

Burns, *Revival Sermons*, Banner of Truth, 1980 (reprint)

Bushman, *The Great Awakening*, Omohundro Institute of Early American History and Culture, 1970

Campbell, *The Price and Power of Revival*, The Faith Mission

Drummond, *Charles Grandison Finney*, Hodder and Stoughton, 1983

Edwards, *Revival, a People Saturated with God*, Evangelical Press, 1990

Jonathan Edwards on Revival, Banner of Truth, 1965

Egerton, *Flame of God*, Ambassador Publications, 1987

Ellsworth, *Come Down Lord*, Banner of Truth, 1988

Evans, *Revival Comes to Wales*, Evangelical Press of Wales, 1959

Evans and Jones, *A Pictorial History of Revival*, CWR, 2004

Fawcett, *The Cambuslang Revival*, Banner of Truth, 1971

Griffin, *The Forgotten Revival*, Day One, 1992

Hughes, *Revival – Times of Refreshing*, CWR 1990

Jones, *Rent Heavens*, Stanley Martin &Co. Ltd. 1930

Koch, *Revival Fires in Canada*, Kregel Publications, 1974

Lloyd-Jones, *Revival-Can we Make It Happen?* Marshall-Pickering, 1986

Lovelace, *Dynamics of Spiritual Life*, IVP, 1979

Mills, *Preparing For Revival*, Kingsway, 1990

Morgan, *The Great Awakening in Wales*, Epworth Press, 1988

Murray, *The Coming Revival*, Marshall-Pickering, 1989

Osborn, *Fire in the Hills,* Highland, 1991

Orr, *The Eager Feet*, Moody Press, 1975

Orr, *The Fervent Prayer*, Moody Press, 1974

Orr, *The Flaming Tongue*, Moody Press, 1973

Paisley, *The Fifty-Nine Revival*, Free Presbyterian Press of Ulster, 1958

Phillips, *The Welsh Revival*, Banner of Truth, 1987

Pratney, *Revival*, Whitaker House, 1983

Penn-Lewis, *The Awakening in Wales*, The Overcomer Trust

Ravenhill, *Revival Praying*, Bethany House, 1979

Ravenhill, *Revival God's Way*, Bethany Hopuse, 1983

Ravenhill, *Why Revival Tarries*, Bethany House, 1987

Roberts, *Revival*, Tyndale House, 1988

Shenton, *A Cornish Revival*, Evangelical Press, 2003

Sprague, *Lectures on Revival*, Banner of Truth, 1958 (first pub. 1832)

Stibbe, *Revival*, Monarch Books, 1998

Tari, *Like a Mighty Wind*, Kingsway, 1971

Tracy, *The Great Awakening*, Banner of Truth, 1976

Wallis, *In The Day of Thy Power*, CLC, 1956

Wallis, *Rain from Heaven*, Hodder and Stoughton, 1979

Weakley (complied by) *The Nature of Revival*, Bethany House 1987

Weir, *Heaven Came Down*, Ambassador Publications, 1987

Whittaker, *Great Revivals*, Marshalls, 1984

Woolsey, *Duncan Campbell*, Hodder and Stoughton, 1974